CW00546211

THE CHALLENGES
OF DEMOCRACY

ALSO BY JONATHAN SUMPTION

Trials of the State
Law in a Time of Crisis

THE CHALLENGES OF DEMOCRACY

AND THE RULE OF LAW

JONATHAN SUMPTION

Profile Books

First published in Great Britain in 2025 by
Profile Books Ltd
29 Cloth Fair
London
ECIA 7JQ
www.profilebooks.com

10 9 8 7 6 5 4 3 2 1

Typeset in Dante by MacGuru Ltd
Printed and bound in Great Britain by
CPI Group (UK) Ltd, Croydon CR0 4YY

A CIP catalogue record for this book is available from the British Library.

ISBN 978 1 80522 250 7
eISBN 978 1 80522 251 4

Contents

I

INTRODUCTION

All but one of the chapters in this volume originated as lectures delivered to a variety of audiences in different places. They are occasional pieces, but there is an underlying theme. Britain, like other European countries, is a democracy. But what does that mean? What are the conditions in which democracy can exist? What part does law play in creating those conditions, or perhaps in extinguishing them? Can democracy survive an age of polarised opinion and hostility to dissent? Will Britain still be a democracy in fifty years' time? Until recently, these questions hardly seemed worth asking. Politics is the essential mechanism of the democratic state, but the disrepute into which politics have fallen, both in Britain and elsewhere, has pushed the travails of democracy to the top of today's agenda. As I write this, in July 2024, disillusionment with democracy and an appetite for authoritarian styles of government is growing across Europe and in the United States. Each succeeding poll points to a declining faith in democratic politics and an overpowering contempt for politicians.

Why has this happened? One view is that our politicians are uniquely vicious, incompetent or corrupt. That is a fair criticism of a very small number of them, but it is plainly not a fair description of the generality of those involved in politics. It seems likely that there are more fundamental causes at work than the supposed failings of the current generation of politicians. Three factors in particular have had an important impact on current perceptions of the political process.

The first is about representation. In spite of the occasional resort to referenda, all modern democracies operate on the basis that the electorate chooses others to make decisions on their behalf, and may remove them at stated intervals if they are dissatisfied. This has advantages that no other system can replicate. It is more likely to achieve long-term stability than direct democracy. It dilutes the electorate's prejudices and enthusiasms which may be short-lived. It tends to marginalise extremes, as representatives try to satisfy the broadest range of opinion in the interest of getting re-elected. Representation disperses power and inhibits its arbitrary exercise. By making office-holders answerable to a permanent body that is broader than their own cronies, representative democracy encourages a more consultative style of decision-making and a more careful approach to the dilemmas that are an inherent part of government. These things usually make for better policymaking. In a representative democracy governments will not necessarily govern well, but they are more likely to govern well than autocrats. These are some of the reasons why we need elites. Democratic elites at least have the advantage that they are answerable to the public at periodic elections, so that no political class can diverge for very long or very fundamentally from the values of the population at large. However, representation inevitably creates a professional political class, and no professional political class can ever be truly representative of its electors. Success in politics requires single-minded ambition and determination. Success in government requires high levels of intelligence, judgement and application. These qualities are uncommon, which means that democracies are in reality removable aristocracies of knowledge. This has sometimes been contemptuously labelled 'bystander democracy'. The eighteenth-century philosopher Jean-Jacques Rousseau had harsh things to say about it. 'The day you elect representatives,' he observed, 'you lose your freedom.' Many people today who have never read *The Social Contract* share Rousseau's instinct. Elites are rarely popular. Contempt for them is one of the oldest tropes of democratic politics.

A second problem is that public expectations are unrealistically high. For most of human history, the main limitation on the power of the state was its ignorance. Since the middle of the nineteenth century, the capacities of government have been transformed. Today's state is characterised by immense bureaucracies, vast resources of information, and elaborate electronic tools for retrieving and filtering it as required. Economic surpluses over subsistence levels have grown so as to make a far higher proportion of personal incomes taxable. It has become possible to direct impressive resources towards collective welfare, as it was not in earlier periods. These changes have coincided with the onset of mass democracy, and have encouraged high hopes for improving the lot of mankind. Yet there are many desirable things that the state cannot achieve. Governments can create the conditions for prosperity and remove artificial barriers to prosperity, but they cannot create prosperity. Governments have proved unable to halt the spread of infectious disease, or even significantly limit it. Governments cannot seal off their borders against illegal immigrants any more than the Roman Empire could stop the Germanic hordes at the Rhine or the Danube. These are merely the most topical examples. There are many others. Politicians are expected to promise the undeliverable and are then damned for failing to deliver it. The result is to undermine the trust in institutions that is indispensable in any state not founded on mere force. The failure of trust is aggravated by a mismatch between the way that the public and ministers think about policy. When the public criticises the government it commonly focuses on one issue at a time: the government has failed to improve outcomes in the National Health Service, or it has failed to resolve the problem of housing shortage, or it has failed to control crime. But governments do not have the luxury of thinking of one thing at a time. Most policy decisions have side effects in other policy areas. Many things that the state can do to address one problem serve to aggravate another. Some things are only deliverable at the expense of other important values such as liberty, acceptable levels of taxation or economic growth.

Thirdly, democracies have proved incapable of dealing with some major modern challenges, precisely because they are democracies. Democratic pressures have stood in the way of potential solutions. Britain faces a severe housing shortage as a result of the failure of housebuilding programmes to keep up with the rate of household formation. The result has been a steep rise in house prices and rents. Even with help from the bank of Mum and Dad, the average age at which people buy their first home outside London has risen from 29 in the 1990s to 33.4 in 2023. In London it has been as high as 36.7 (in 2019). The main problems are the planning system and environmental regulation. The planning system makes it too easy to block development in the interest of protecting the amenities of existing home-owners. Recent attempts to reform the planning system hit the buffers in June 2021 when the Conservatives lost a 'safe' home counties seat at Amersham in which the reforms were a major issue. Building houses would be easier without environmental regulation, but this is a classic case of inconsistent goods. We can only solve one problem at the cost of generating another.

Housing is not the only example. The welfare budget disproportionately favours pensioners. The 'triple lock' requires annual increases in pensions significantly more generous than the benefits enjoyed by people of working age. Rising expectation of life means that society has to support a growing proportion of economically inactive citizens. The result is an inexorable increase in the cost of these benefits as a proportion of both public expenditure and GDP. In the long run, this will represent an unsustainable burden on younger generations whose taxes pay for it. Any solution to the problem will be electorally unpopular, especially among older voters who are assiduous voters and have for many years been the mainstay of the Conservative Party. In May 2017, the Conservative election manifesto proposed some relatively modest changes to the system of public provision for the care costs of those living at home. The cost would have been recoverable from the value of their homes after their death, as already happened for the costs of those in care homes. This was promptly labelled a 'dementia tax' and the party was forced to abandon the scheme. The incident is thought to have contributed significantly to the loss of its parliamentary majority on polling day. These problems are not peculiar to Britain. In France, President Macron increased the retiring age in order to make the provision of pensions financially sustainable, but the change provoked strikes, riots and cost him his electoral base. He now faces a National Assembly dominated by both left and right extremes that are agreed on only one thing – the repeal of his pension reforms. As a former President of the European Commission observed about the eurozone crisis of 2009–10, 'We all know what we have to do, but we just don't know how to get re-elected when we have done it.'

Climate change is probably the most significant issue on which democratic pressures inhibit effective solutions. It seems beyond question that some measures will have to be taken to curb emissions if life on this planet is to remain tolerable. The longer that these measures are delayed, the more expensive and intrusive they will have to be. Earlier environmental concerns, such as those surrounding the use of pesticides and other pollutants, called for measures that did not significantly affect standards of living. But dealing with climate change will almost certainly involve reducing consumption, which will be hard to sell in a democracy. The electoral kickback has already begun. In Britain, measures to phase out the uses of hydrocarbon fuels for heating have been postponed in response to public hostility. In Germany, electoral politics are leading to the phasing out of one of the main sources of clean energy, namely nuclear power. A major populist party, Alternativ für Deutschland, has garnered significant electoral support by denying that any climate crisis exists. The Netherlands, much of which is below sea level, is probably more vulnerable to climate change than any other European country, but hostility to measures to deal with it has boosted the electoral prospects of extremists who promise to resist them. In France, plans to increase fuel taxes and reduce speed limits on motorways were greeted with riots and ultimately abandoned. In the United States, Donald Trump is campaigning on a programme of boosting oil production and taking an axe to most of the measures taken by American governments to date to curb emissions.

In Britain, these problems have opened up a dangerous political gap between generations. Housing shortage, pension provision and climate change are all examples of major issues on which the interests of older and younger generations conflict. This is part of a wider pattern in which opinion is polarised between generations on a range of issues: Brexit, student loans, immigration, racial tension, transgender rights, Gaza and many more. Support for centre-right and right-wing parties has always tended to increase with age, but the current (June 2024) figures are more extreme than they have ever been. In the general election of July 2024, only 8 per cent of voters aged under thirty voted Conservative, and another 10 per cent voted Reform UK. The only age group in which right-of-centre parties commanded a majority were the over-sixties. Surveys of opinion such as those published in 2020 by the Bennett Institute in Cambridge or in 2023 by the Open Society Foundation, all suggest that disillusionment with democracy is strongest among younger citizens. They are much more dissatisfied than their elders were at the same stage in life, and the situation is getting worse. This is reflected in their growing interest in anti-democratic methods of political expression. Climate change is once again the clearest illustration. Climate change activists, who are mostly young, are resorting to tactics designed not to persuade but to inconvenience a public seen to be indifferent or lukewarm to their cause. They are an expression of frustrated outrage at the failure of democratic politics to accommodate their views. A climate protester recently jailed for climbing onto the Dartford Bridge and forcing police to close it for several hours argued in an interview with the *Guardian* that disruption was necessary because persuasion had not worked. 'Politics as usual was not going to deliver,' he is quoted as saying. For protesters, no process of collective decision-making can be legitimate if it might lead to any other outcome than the one that they support. This is an essentially autocratic outlook and an implicit rejection of the democratic process. If an important, identifiable sector of the population is consistently marginalised on major issues affecting them, this will happen more often.

Democracy has a natural tendency to create interest groups for whom the preservation of their current advantages or the acquisition of new ones are the dominant factors in their political choices. It is asking a lot to expect people to look beyond their own interest at the broader interests of society and to future problems that may not materialise until after their death. Historical experience is not encouraging. But if democracy is to survive, a higher political morality may be required not just of politicians but of those who elect them. This is a big thing to ask, but it may be in their interest, for unless it happens we are likely to move to a much more autocratic model of government.

Democracy is fragile. It requires what political philosophers from Aristotle onwards have called 'virtue', an ability to put common interests above personal ones. It requires a degree of tolerance and cooperative empathy that is not natural to mankind, especially when opinion on major issues is as polarised as it is today in many major democracies. It depends on a culture that takes decades, even centuries, to take root but that can be destroyed quite quickly. These are some of the reasons why democracy is a relatively recent creation whose survival cannot be taken for granted. In Britain, universal male franchise is barely 150 years old. Women did not get the vote on the same terms as men until 1928. In France it did not happen until 1946. Today, democracy is very far from being the default condition of mankind. The Economist Intelligence Unit, which has published a Democracy Index since 2006, reckons that in 2022 only 24 of the 167 countries covered, with 8 per cent of the world's population, ranked as full democracies, down from 28 in 2006. Britain was one of them. In many countries, ostensibly democratic institutions have been imperceptibly emptied of everything that made them democratic. The world is full of autocracies that grew out of democracies without any criminal or illegal conduct, when authoritarian groups manipulated the distribution of favours and penalties, took control of state broadcasting organisations and 'regulated' private media, harassed potential opponents, exploited gaps in the constitution and rode roughshod over political conventions. Venezuela under Chavez and Hungary under Orbán are good examples. Many countries, including important ones like Russia and China, have never been democracies. Their leaders have publicly expressed their contempt for the political systems of Western liberal democracies. 'Democracy is not our tradition', said a spokesman for the Hong Kong government quite recently. The United States is one of the world's oldest democracies, but its recent history shows how easy it is for even a sophisticated modern state to slide into autocracy. Donald Trump has openly expressed his admiration for Vladimir Putin, Xi Jinping and Kim Jong Un. Today, the United States counts as only a 'flawed democracy' in the *Economist's* tables. By some definitions, nearly three-quarters of the world's population today live under authoritarian regimes of one kind or another. Will Britain be one of them?

POLITICS AND THE STATE

II

DEMOCRACY AND ITS ENEMIES*

Towards the end of his long life John Adams, one of the founding fathers of American democracy, became increasingly gloomy about its prospects. Writing to the Virginia politician John Taylor in 1814, he observed that 'democracy never lasts long. It soon wastes, exhausts and murders itself. There never was a democracy yet that did not commit suicide.' When Adams chose the word 'suicide' to describe the death of democracies, he was not just resorting to a dramatic turn of phrase. He was making a deliberate and important point. Democracies fail from within. They are not usually overwhelmed by external forces such as invasion or insurrection. They fail because people spontaneously turn to more authoritarian forms of government. Adams had in mind the

---

*This is a slightly expanded version of a lecture originally delivered in October 2021 at the Sheldonian Theatre in Oxford in memory of Roger Scruton. Scruton was one of the most original minds of our time. He was commonly described as a conservative. But he was not a party man, and it would have been more accurate to call him a traditionalist. He believed in the organic development of human societies, and in the cumulative wisdom which humanity derives from its past. Scruton was a romantic, but he was not just a romantic. He was an intensely rational thinker, who deployed reason to great effect but he also understood the limits to what reason could achieve. He was also, of course, many other things: a fine musician, an elegant writer, a fierce horseman, a good friend, a wise counsellor and a devoted husband and father. I wish that I could have submitted the text to him in draft for his comments, but as it is, I offer it to honour his life now that it has ended.

democracies of the ancient world, the only precedents available before the foundation of the United States. According to the orthodox narrative, the democracies of the ancient world had died because people succumbed to the appeal of demagogues, who promised them security at home and triumphs abroad in return for their acceptance of autocracy. People simply lost interest in democratic government. John Adams's sombre prediction did not come true in his own day. But is it becoming true in ours?

The Pew Research Centre has been tracking attitudes to democracy in different countries for some thirty years. Dissatisfaction with democracy has been rising in advanced democracies for most of that time. This is especially true of young people living in the oldest democracies: the United States, the United Kingdom and France. In a recent survey, the United Kingdom was found to have had one of the highest levels of dissatisfaction in the world, at 69 per cent. It seems that only the Bulgarians and the Greeks think less of democracy than the British. Of course, dissatisfaction with democracy does not necessarily imply a preference for some other system. But more disturbing findings emerge from the regular surveys of political engagement conducted in Britain by the Hansard Society. In the 2019 survey, 54 per cent of respondents agreed with the statement that 'Britain needs a strong leader willing to break the rules'. Only 23 per cent disagreed. Nearly half of those who agreed wanted a strong leader willing to break the rules. They thought that such a person 'shouldn't have to worry so much about votes in Parliament'. Polling evidence is not infallible, but these polls track attitudes over a considerable period of time, and indicate the direction in which we are travelling. They are consistent with the historically high levels of electoral support for authoritarian figures such as Donald Trump, Marine Le Pen, Jörg Haider and the leading lights of Alternativ für Deutschland.

The first question that we need to ask is what we mean by democracy. We are so familiar with its use as a general term of approval that some definition seems necessary. What I mean by the word is a constitutional mechanism for collective self-government. Democracy is a way of entrusting decision-making to people acceptable to the majority, whose power is defined and limited, and whose mandate is revocable. That is the institutional framework. But the institutional framework is not enough. Plenty of countries have the institutional framework of a democracy without being one. This is because democracy can only work in a legal and social culture where there is freedom of thought, speech and association, uncontrolled access to reliable information, and a large tolerance of political dissent. A culture of this kind is vulnerable. Where democracies fail, it is not usually because the institutional framework has failed. It is because the necessary cultural foundation has collapsed. The opposite of democracy is some form of authoritarian government. It is of course possible for democracies to confer considerable coercive power on the state without losing their democratic character. It has happened in wartime, and it happened more recently during the Covid-19 pandemic. But there is a point beyond which the systematic application of coercion is no longer consistent with any notion of collective self-government. The fact that it is hard to define where that point lies does not mean that there isn't one. A degree of respect for individual autonomy seems to me to be a necessary feature of anything that deserves to be called a democracy.

The chief enemies of democracy are economic insecurity, intolerance and fear.

Let me first address economic insecurity. Historically, democracies have always been heavily dependent on economic optimism. Except for two short periods, the United States has until quite recently enjoyed continuously rising levels of prosperity, both in absolute terms and relative to other countries. Britain's economic history, like that of other European countries, has been more chequered. But the trajectory has generally been upward. Sixty years of post-war expansion have raised those expectations to a very high level. Today, the outlook is darker. We face problems of faltering growth, relative economic decline, redundant skills and capricious patterns of inequality. These symptoms are particularly acute in Britain, where they are aggravated by historically low productivity, poor levels of investment, and self-inflicted wounds such as an ill-conceived and badly managed departure from the European Union and a highly destructive response to the pandemic. The consciousness of Britain's past economic greatness makes the impact of these problems that much greater. In most Western democracies, including ours, gross domestic product is still rising, albeit slowly. But people measure their well-being against their expectations. The shattering of optimism is therefore a dangerous moment in the life of any community. Disillusionment with the promise of progress was a major factor in the thirty-year crisis of Europe which began in 1914 and ended in 1945. That crisis was characterised by a resort to totalitarianism in much of Europe. Britain, the United States and France escaped that fate, but in all three countries, there were powerful authoritarian movements of left and right that drew their strength mainly from economic misfortune. Russia and Germany were widely regarded as the models that showed the way out, just as totalitarian China was until very recently.

Economic insecurity has another potentially disruptive consequence. It heightens concerns about inequality. Hostility to great fortunes and especially to new ones is natural to mankind and always has been. It was a perennial theme of the politics of the ancient world. Seven centuries ago Dante placed the new rich in one of the lower pits of hell. Yet inequality is an inevitable consequence of liberty. It reflects the diversity, energy, ambition and enthusiasm of disparate human beings in any society in which these qualities are not artificially suppressed. In particular, it is a natural consequence of innovation, which is a necessary condition of economic growth but inevitably disrupts the existing distribution of income and wealth. Those who perceive and exploit new economic opportunities will almost always fare better than their fellows. This is one reason why the United States, with the world's most dynamic economy, is also among the world's most unequal societies. I do not accept the various theories, which writers like Thomas Piketty and Brett Christophers have made fashionable, which underrate the dynamic quality of economic life and attribute inequality mainly to institutional factors or the leaden legacies of the past. But there are legitimate concerns about fortunes made by activities that have no discernable economic value or those that are due to market distortions or the exploitation of social goods. Economic misfortune bears hardest on the poorest members of society. Extremes of inequality can be socially disruptive, promoting resentments that undermine the sense of shared identity that is the foundation of any democracy. Whether inequality has reached anything like that level in Britain is a controversial question. I doubt it. By most measures, inequality in Britain is broadly in line with other western European countries and well below the world average. What is clear is that when growth falters people become more interested in the distribution of income and wealth. This can poison democratic politics whether it is justified or not.

The second of democracy's great enemies is fear. People who are sufficiently frightened will submit to an authoritarian regime that offers them security against some real or imagined threat. Historically, the threat has usually been war. In the two world wars of the twentieth century Britain transformed itself into a temporary despotism with substantial public support. Wars, however, are rare. This country has generally conducted its wars at a distance. It has not faced an existential threat from external enemies since 1940. The real threat to democracy's survival is not major disasters like war. It is comparatively minor perils that in the nature of things occur more frequently. This may seem paradoxical. But it must be obvious that the more routine the perils from which we demand protection from the state, the more frequently will those demands arise. If we confer despotic powers on government to deal with perils that are an ordinary feature of human existence, we will end up doing it most or all of the time. Because the demand for security has grown dramatically in modern democracies, the perils against which we now demand protection are more numerous than they were. This is likely to lead to a more fundamental and durable change in our attitudes to the state. It is a more serious problem for the future of democracy than war.

This has happened because of the growing aversion of Western societies to risk. We crave protection from many risks that are inherent in life itself: financial loss, economic insecurity, crime, sexual violence and abuse, sickness, accidental injury. Even the Covid-19 pandemic, serious as it was, was well within the broad range of mortal diseases with which human beings have always had to live. We call upon the state to save us from these things. This is not irrational. It is in some ways a natural response to the remarkable increase in the technical competence of mankind since the middle of the nineteenth century, which has considerably increased the range of things that the state can do. For all perils, there must be a governmental solution. If there is none, that implies a lack of governmental competence. Attitudes to death provide a striking example. There are few things as routine as death. 'In the midst of life, we are in death', says *The Book of Common Prayer*. Yet the technical possibilities of modern, publicly financed medicine have accustomed us to the idea that except in extreme old age, any death from disease is premature, and that all premature death is avoidable. Starting as a natural event, death has become a symptom of societal failure. In modern conditions, risk aversion and the fear that goes with it, are a standing invitation to authoritarian government. If we hold governments responsible for everything that goes wrong, they will take away our autonomy so that nothing can go wrong. In Britain, we had had a spectacular demonstration of this during the pandemic, when coercive measures with radical effects on our lives were made by ministers with strong public support but minimal parliamentary input. Whatever one thinks about this, it unquestionably marks a significant change in our collective mentality.

The quest for security at the price of coercive state intervention is a feature of democratic politics which was pointed out in the 1830s by the great political scientist Alexis de Toqueville in his remarkable study of American democracy, a book whose uncanny relevance still takes one by surprise even after nearly two centuries. His description of the process cannot be bettered. The protecting power of the state, he wrote:

> extends its arm over the whole community. It covers the surface of society with complicated rules, minute and uniform, through which the most original minds and the most energetic characters cannot penetrate, to rise above the crowd. The will of man is not shattered. But it is softened, bent, and guided. Men are seldom forced to act, but they are constantly restrained from acting. Such a power does not destroy, but it prevents existence; it does not tyrannize, but it compresses, enervates, extinguishes. It

stupefies a people until each nation is reduced to nothing better than a flock of timid and industrious animals, of which the government is the shepherd.

This brings me to the problem of intolerance or, as we call it when it reaches a sufficient scale, polarisation. In many ways, the biggest threat to democracy is not oppression by the state, but the intolerance of our fellow citizens. In the early years of British democracy, the great apostle of Victorian liberalism John Stuart Mill foresaw that the main threat to its survival would be the conformity imposed by public opinion. Roger Scruton once wrote that 'the freedom to entertain and express opinions, however offensive ... [is] the precondition of a political society.' Scruton had more personal experience of this than any of us. He was a persistent and joyful dissentient. In the same article, he identified the problem with unerring accuracy. To guarantee freedom of opinion,' he wrote, 'goes against the grain of social life, and imposes risks that people may be reluctant to take. For in criticising orthodoxy, you are not just questioning a belief – you are threatening the social order that has been built on it.'

The deliberate campaigns of suppression conducted by pressure groups against politically unfashionable or 'incorrect' opinions on, for example, race, gender reassignment or same-sex relationships, the attempts to impose a new vocabulary that implicitly accepts the campaigners' point of view, these things are symptoms of the narrowing of our intellectual world. The tests recently imposed on freshers at the University of St Andrews and the campaign against Kathleen Stock at the University of Sussex suggest that intellectual persecution is alive even in our universities, for the first time, perhaps, since Thomas Cranmer was burned at the stake just 200 yards from the Sheldonian Theatre. Demonstrations, such as those organised by Extinction Rebellion and Insulate

Britain, are based on the notion that the campaigners' point of view is the only legitimate one. It is therefore perfectly acceptable deliberately to bully people and disrupt their lives until they submit, instead of resorting to ordinary democratic procedures. This is the mentality of terrorists, but without the violence. Democracy can only survive if our differences are transcended by our common acceptance of the legitimacy of the decision-making process, even when we disagree profoundly with the outcome. This implicit bargain breaks down if people feel more strongly about the issues than they do about democratic procedures for settling them. The result is the abandonment of political engagement and a growing resort to direct action of one kind or another.

Direct action is an invitation to authoritarian government, because it implicitly rejects diversity of opinion. It assesses the value of democratic institutions by one criterion only, namely the degree to which the activists' programme has prevailed. Those who engage in direct action instinctively feel that the end is so important that it justifies the means, but they rarely confront the implications of their acts. Since we are never likely to agree on controversial issues of principle, what holds us together is not consensus, but a common respect for a method of resolving our differences, whether or not we approve of the result. Conflicts of opinion and interest are natural features of any free society. The task of a political community is to accommodate them so that we can live together in peace without systematic coercion. This is necessarily a political process, which is why the contempt for politics expressed by so many activists is potentially a mortal threat to our democracy.

The successive surveys of the Hansard Society paint a picture of a society in which interest in public affairs is strong, but people are unwilling to engage actively in politics. The Conservative Party has been the dominant party of government for the past century. Yet its membership has declined from about 2.8 million in the mid-1950s to about 170,000 according to the latest estimates. Labour Party membership is larger, at about 430,000, but still a long way below its earlier peak. This pattern is fairly typical internationally. The membership rolls of established political parties has declined steeply in most European democracies. By comparison, support for new parties dedicated to the wholesale rejection of normal party politics has increased, jerkily but noticeably: in France La République en Marche (as it was originally called), in Italy the Five Star Movement, in Spain Podemos and Reform UK in Britain have all in their day presented themselves as representatives of a new electorate, and as spontaneous expressions of the popular will rather than traditional political parties. Podemos has declared that there is no left or right. There is only 'the people', identified with Podemos itself, versus 'the caste', i.e. professional politicians. In Italy, the Five Star Movement claimed not to be a political party but a movement, and promoted direct democracy with electronic voting. Remarkably, lack of political experience was a central part of the successful candidates' pitch in the US presidential election of 2016, the French presidential election of 2017 and the Italian legislative elections of 2018.

These facts reflect a fundamental problem about democracy, which was pointed out more than two millennia ago by Aristotle. Aristotle regarded professional politics as an evil because he thought that it created a political elite that would end up serving its own interests. This has been the received opinion for centuries, right up to Noam Chomsky and beyond. In my experience it is untrue, at any rate in Britain. Professional politicians can never be intellectually pure. They are constrained by the need to compromise in order to build majorities. But almost all of them are public-spirited individuals with a genuine ambition to serve their country. They would acquire a great deal more money and status by pursuing other careers. Nevertheless, the old trope that politicians are a bunch of corrupt, self-interested and power-crazed hypocrites is deeply embedded in the public mind and always has been. Aristotle's solution was to abolish the political class and replace it with a system in which public offices would be held for short periods by men chosen by lot or serving in rotation. Everyone can then feel that they are at least potentially engaged in a system of self-government. This is hardly realistic in an electorate of some 47 million. But Aristotle had put his finger on the reason why many people reject democracy. They feel alienated from the political class that democracies inevitably generate. They do not regard politicians as representative of themselves, even if they voted for them. There is no cure for this condition. Successful politicians are in the nature of things unlikely to be representative of the electorate. They require an altogether exceptional degree of ambition, application and intellect. Those who are in government have to apply themselves to complex issues with an intensity for which most of us have neither time nor inclination. If one object of representative politics is to choose politicians who are best-qualified to perform the exceptionally difficult job of governing, then our representatives will always be unrepresentative.

None of this has stopped enthusiasts for constitutional innovation from exploring a variety of ways in which to sideline the political class. Referenda are one possibility, but Britain's experience with referenda has not been entirely happy. They only work if people are voting about precise proposals (necessarily formulated by politicians) whose acceptance or rejection by the electorate will resolve the whole issue. Otherwise, they are simply the prelude to further rounds of political infighting. The referenda on Scottish independence in 2014 and Brexit in 2016 perfectly illustrate the problem. Citizens' assemblies are currently the favourite proposals for circumventing professional politics. They are the modern equivalent of Aristotle's selection by lot. They seek to introduce into our constitutional arrangements a succession of ad hoc focus groups. But there are a number of problems about this approach to decision-making. The first concerns the selection of the participants. They are usually chosen on the assumption that people of a given socio-economic class or level of education will be politically representative of the categories to which they belong. That assumption seems likely to be wrong. Groups such as manual workers, members of particular ethnic groups or over-sixty-fives, for example, are no more uniform or consistent in their political opinions than the electorate at large. It is therefore largely a matter of accident whether our divisions are replicated in a citizen's assembly of, say, one hundred people. They have not been chosen by the electorate and are not answerable to anyone. They therefore have no democratic legitimacy. Secondly, citizens' assemblies by definition lack the experience that enables professional politicians to assess what they are being told. They are heavily dependent on the expert advisers who endeavour to analyse the options and their consequences. The system is too vulnerable to manipulation and facile solutions. Thirdly, they are generally invited to consider one issue at a time and to choose the best of a number of available options. But government is not like that. Problems crowd in on decision-makers all at once. Potential solutions compete for finite resources. They inter-react. The best solution to one problem may seriously aggravate another. The quest is not always for the best or most popular option, but for the least bad, something perhaps that nobody wants but most people can live with.

There are measures that might palliate the current problems of democracy, but without solving them. Foremost among them is proportional representation. Proportional representation would probably create a multiplicity of political parties. That would more fairly reflect the diversity of opinion among the electorate than the current system. For the same reason it might also increase popular participation in the political process. It is probably the system that we would choose if we were building a constitution from scratch. But first past the post is the system that we have inherited, and the power of inertia in a complex and stable society is such that we are probably stuck with it. Proportional representation would be contrary to the interests of the two major national parties and there is no real demand for it among the electorate. The alternative vote referendum of 2011 suggests that the British prefer the crude simplicity of the first-past-the-post system to anything more elaborate. Recent polling evidence points to the same conclusion. It is fair to say that proportional representation would do nothing to address the alienation of the electorate from the political process. Indeed, it might well increase it, since it would lead to less stable governments and more political infighting.

I am not about to suggest my own solution to Aristotle's problem with professional politics, because I do not believe that there is one. Whatever we may think of our politicians, it is an inescapable truth that we cannot have democracy without politics or politics without politicians. We have to learn to accept the vices and virtues of professional politics, because they are inherent in the whole nature of government. Getting rid of professional politics would almost certainly lead to the replacement of the current political elite by a different one that would be more permanent, more authoritarian and less representative. Ultimately all political systems are aristocracies of knowledge. Democracies are no different, except that the aristocracies of the moment are removable.

A generation ago, the enemies of democracy were small groups of cranks and extremists of left and right. But today democracy needs a coherent defence, not just against those who would like to dispense with it in favour of more authoritarian models, but against those who would like to redefine it out of existence. We have to have something to say to the 54 per cent of our fellow citizens who would apparently prefer to be ruled by a British Putin. Why are they wrong? The simplest thing to be said against them is that democracy is an efficient way of getting rid of unsatisfactory governments without violence. But there are at least three other, more profound reasons why people living in a country like ours ought to believe in democracy.

In the first place, it is the best protection that we have for liberty. Since a large measure of individual autonomy is a necessary condition for human happiness and creativity, this is a consideration of some importance. I am well aware of the oppressive possibilities of democracy. I do not doubt that democracy has the potential to oppress not just ethnic or social minorities, but political or moral minorities, people who believe something that majorities object to. That was pointed out by Madison and Mill at the birth of modern democracy, and indeed by Aristotle more than twenty centuries before that. In most periods of history, the best guarantee of liberty has been the powerlessness and ignorance of the state. Historically, it was relatively easy to escape its scrutiny, and take shelter in the domain of private life. The immense power of the modern state and its almost unlimited access to information makes it harder for us to hide. Access to the levers of state power by democratic majorities is therefore potentially more dangerous today than it has ever been. But democracy at least offers the possibility of redemption. Its values can be turned against those currently in power. By comparison, authoritarian states entrench themselves in power. They institutionalise repression and cultural control in a way that is more difficult to reverse.

Secondly, the creation of a political class, which Aristotle regarded as the great vice of democracy, may well be its chief merit. Political parties operate in what I have previously called the political market. They are coalitions of opinion, united by a loose consistency of outlook and the desire to win elections. To command a parliamentary majority, parties have traditionally had to bid for support from a highly diverse electorate. Their policy offerings mutate in response to changes in the public's sentiments that seem likely to influence voting patterns. Their whole object is to produce a slate of policies that perhaps only a minority would have chosen as their preferred option, but which the broadest possible range of people can live with. This has traditionally made them powerful engines of national compromise and effective mediators between the state and the electorate. It has also served as a good protection against extremes. Autocracy, by comparison, offers no protection at all against extremes.

Thirdly, democracy is usually more efficient. There is a common delusion, which I suspect is shared by many of the 54 per cent, that strongmen get things done. They do not waste time in argument or debate. Historical experience should warn us against this idea, which is almost always wrong. The concentration of power in a small number of hands and the absence of wider deliberation and scrutiny enables authoritarian governments to make major decisions on the hoof, without proper forethought, planning, research or consultation. Within the government's ranks, it promotes loyalty at the expense of wisdom, flattery at the expense of objective advice, and self-interest at the expense of the public interest. The want of criticism encourages self-confidence, and self-confidence banishes moderation and restraint. The opacity of authoritarian governments is a standing invitation to corruption.

These have always been the main advantages of representative democracy, and they are just as obvious today. But will they prevail? I am a natural optimist, but I have to say that I am not optimistic about the future of democracy, in this country or elsewhere in the West. All of the threats to democracy that I have discussed above seem likely to intensify in the coming years. The public attitudes that I have been talking about are all too natural to human beings. Democracy has existed for barely two centuries in Europe and the United States, less in other places. It was the creation of an exceptional combination of political and cultural factors, which would never have been easy to sustain and whose impact is now fading. The craving for security is too deeply embedded in human nature to go away. Fear will never lose its capacity to distort our collective judgements. The decline of political tolerance and the rise of moral absolutism are trends which are just as unlikely to be reversed.

The major challenge to democracy in the coming years will, I believe, be climate change. Climate change is likely to be the main generator of collective fear in the decades to come and quite possibly the main temptation to direct action. It is of course possible that we will do nothing very much about climate change and simply chug along dealing locally with the consequences as and when they arise. But I do not doubt that more radical measures to deal with climate change are necessary. On the assumption that some action is taken, it is likely to run into strong democratic headwinds. Most of the measures needed to deal with climate change involve reducing consumption and curtailing economic growth. This will not be popular and may not be accepted by democratic electorates, especially if groups come forward to offer easier and perhaps specious alternatives. Climate change can only effectually be dealt with at an international level. This will require major decisions to be made internationally, in a world where lines of democratic accountability are still national. Democracy requires a common loyalty to the decision-making process, which is strong enough to transcend people's disagreements about particular issues. That depends on a common sense of identity and a large measure of mutual solidarity. At the moment, this sense of solidarity exists, if at all, only at the level of the nation state. We have had a stark reminder of that in the Brexit referendum.

Perhaps in future, climate change will generate a measure of international solidarity that will resolve this problem, but I would not count on it. National identities are becoming stronger, and climate change is likely to make them stronger still. This is because although all humanity has a common interest in dealing with climate change, they do not have a common interest in the measures necessary to do it. We have seen this on issues like fossil fuels and deforestation. Countries like India, China, Malaysia and Brazil, are not likely to accept measures that will restrict their ability to achieve the same standard of living as the West. Especially when they reflect that historically the West has to some degree achieved that standard of living by polluting the world. Countries like the United States and Britain are not likely to accept a disproportionate reduction of their own standard of living as the price of international agreement. The logical outcome of the threat of climate change is not international harmony in the face of a common danger. It is a world of competitive despotisms.

The transition from democracy to authoritarian rule is generally smooth and unnoticed. It is easy to sleepwalk into it. The outward forms and the language of politics are unchanged. But the substance is gone. These things do not happen with a clap of thunder. Democracy is not formally abolished but quietly redefined. It ceases to be a method of government, and becomes instead a set of political values, like communism or human rights, which are said to represent the people's true wishes without regard to anything that they may actually have chosen for themselves. Historically, the default position of human societies has always been some form of autocracy. The world is full of countries which have reverted to type. The democratic label is still on the bottle but the substance has been poured out of it by governments, usually with substantial public support. Chile, Peru, Venezuela, Brazil, Hungary, Egypt, Turkey, Russia: the list gets longer every year. Will Britain end up on that list? A generation ago, it would have seemed strange even to ask the question, but it is now a real issue.

III

WHAT IS GOING ON IN THE UNITED KINGDOM?*

Looking back on a tumultuous decade, 2012–2022

A lot has happened in British politics in the last ten years. There have been two major referenda. Scottish independence narrowly failed to obtain majority support in the referendum of 2014. Two years later, an even narrower majority called for Britain to leave the European Union, as we have now done. We have had many changes of government in a short time. Britain has been a byword for political stability for three centuries, the polar opposite, in a European context, of Italy. Yet in 2022, we had as many prime ministers in four months as Italy had had in four years.

The events of the past decade are sometimes described as a constitutional crisis, but they really marked a crisis of the party system, and in particular a crisis of the Conservative Party. The Conservative Party governed Britain from

---

In 2022 and 2023, British politics provided an unedifying spectacle to the world, which I was occasionally asked to explain to puzzled observers at home and abroad. My response has been through a number of iterations, as events have unfolded. This version originated in a lecture delivered at Queens' College, Cambridge in July 2023 to the biennial Cambridge seminar of the Canadian Institute, a gathering of judges and senior lawyers from Canada. I have updated it in the light of events since then.

2010 to 2024 and indeed for most of the two centuries since it emerged in something like its present form in the early nineteenth century. In its heyday, it was one of the most successful election-winning machines in the world. It represented an important strand in British political thinking: pragmatic, moderate, competent, patriotic and non-ideological, suspicious of the overreaching state and disruptive change, but open to evolutionary reform. This combination has had considerable appeal to its major constituencies: business people great and small, the more prosperous members of what used to be called the working class, and metropolitan liberals. The Conservative Party has survived as long as it has because it is a chameleon. It is not so much a political platform as an attitude of mind, which is capable of accommodating many different political platforms. It subtly changes its offering in response to perceived changes in public sentiment. All political parties do that, but historically the Conservative Party has done it more successfully for longer than any other party in the Western world.

Crises of the party system are the natural consequence of the process of adaptation to change that all long-standing political parties undergo in a democracy. Before the Second World War, there were many such crises, involving major shifts in the parliamentary tectonic plates. Irish Home Rule and imperial tariff preference before the First World War, the attempt of Lloyd George to cling to power in the 1920s, and the crash of 1929 all generated political crises that dissolved party loyalties and destabilised governments. Earlier generations had experienced similar crises in the eighteenth and nineteenth centuries, provoked by disputes over, for example, the British response to the French revolutionary wars at the dawn of the nineteenth century, Catholic emancipation in the 1820s and 1830s, and the repeal of the Corn Laws in the mid-1840s. Crises like these were once the stuff of politics. In a sense we have simply reverted to an earlier norm.

Many of the major crises of party politics in our history have been about trade policy. And so it is today. The issue that has loosened party loyalties in our own time is Brexit. Brexit is the modern equivalent of the parliamentary crises provoked by the Corn Laws, which nearly destroyed the Conservative Party in the 1840s, and imperial tariff preference, which nearly destroyed the Liberal Party in the 1890s. The Conservatives had brought Britain into the European Community in 1973, at a time when hostility to Europe was concentrated on the left. But the party's traditional support for Europe began to erode during the 1980s, when the European Community moved into the area of social policy and appeared to threaten the small-state model in which most conservatives believed. By the first decade of the present century, the rise of the anti-European UK Independence Party was eating into the Conservative Party's political base. It forced its then leader David Cameron to promise a referendum on Europe in the party's manifesto for the general election of 2015. He expected to win the referendum campaign and believed that that would lay the whole issue to rest for at least a generation. As we now know, that was a miscalculation. He lost the referendum of 2016, provoking the worst political crisis since the Second World War. Even if he had won it, the issue would not have been laid to rest.

The underlying problem is a growing radicalisation of both major national parties at constituency level. Originally, the constituency associations of British political parties were relatively powerless. Their members contributed funding and hard work, but political direction came from the leadership of the parliamentary party. Arthur Balfour, who was Conservative prime minister from 1902 to 1905, is said to have declared that he would rather take political advice from his valet than from rank and file members of his party. In the past century, however, the rank and file of British political parties have acquired considerable power. They choose the local party's candidate in general elections, subject to an ill-defined right of veto by the central party organisation. More recently, they have also achieved a decisive voice in the choice of the party leader. Conservative leaders were chosen by the party's MPs until 2001, when the final choice was transferred to party members in the constituencies. Labour MPs chose their leader until 1981. After some unsatisfactory experiments with an electoral college, Labour handed the choice to party members and supporters in 2015.

These changes have had an important impact on British politics. Until the 1960s and 1970s, people joined political parties for a variety of reasons. Politics was only one of them. At grassroots level, politics had an important social dimension. There were Conservative, Labour and Liberal clubs whose members were united by a common allegiance to the party but whose activities were more social than political. In the early 1950s, political parties were the largest membership organisations in Britain. As I noted in the introduction to this volume, the Conservative Party had about 2.8 million members. Its youth branch, the Young Conservatives, was one of the largest youth movements in the democratic world, and by reputation the best dating agency in the country. The Labour Party had about 1 million members, in addition to the notional membership of those belonging to its affiliated trade unions. In policy terms, the two major parties were broad churches. Between them, they probably represented a rough cross-section of the voting public. Changing patterns of sociability in the age of television and the internet have done away with all that. We drink, talk and consume entertainment at home, not in clubs or other political groups. There has been a steep fall in the membership rolls of all political parties. Today the Conservative Party has only about 170,000 members, a twentieth of its membership at its peak and the Young Conservatives are a much diminished force. The other parties have experienced a similar decline.

The result is that membership of political parties has been abandoned to small numbers of activists who join just for the politics. They are increasingly unrepresentative of those who vote for their party, let alone the wider electorate. Activists naturally congregate at the edges of the political spectrum. This has produced a profound schism between parliamentary parties and their local constituency associations. MPs are there to represent the interests of their constituents and, in a broader sense, the public interest. They will look mainly to the impact of their decisions on the electorate at large, because that will determine their chances of re-election. They know that this will involve a large measure of ideological compromise. By comparison, party members represent no one but themselves. They are inclined to look no further than their own political positions. They are rarely interested in ideological compromise. They will choose candidates and party leaders who share their prejudices, and kid themselves that the rest of the electorate will see the light.

When, in 2001, the Conservatives transferred the choice of leader from MPs to members, the result was the election of Iain Duncan Smith, who was supported by a minority of Tory MPs but by nearly two-thirds of members. The MPs booted him out two years later in a vote of no confidence. In 2015, Labour Party members and supporters nearly destroyed their party by selecting as their leader Jeremy Corbyn, a man in their own image but with little support in the parliamentary party. He had barely achieved the minimum number of endorsements from MPs to present himself as a candidate but he was carried to victory by the votes of constituency members, many of whom joined especially to vote for him. The Parliamentary Labour Party spent four years in an unsuccessful attempt to get rid of him. When Boris Johnson lost the support of his MPs in 2022, the constituency membership of the Conservative Party forced on MPs the catastrophic figure of Liz Truss, who had only limited support in the parliamentary party and lasted just six weeks before she too was thrown out. At one point, it seemed possible that the membership would replace her by reinstating Boris Johnson. Johnson himself was up for it, but a sufficient number of Conservative MPs made it clear that they would not serve in another Johnson government or support it in the House of Commons. Subsequently, a parliamentary committee with a majority of Conservative members unanimously found him to have deliberately lied to Parliament on a number of occasions and triggered the chain of events that led to his leaving Parliament.

In Britain, the first-past-the-post electoral system makes it practically impossible to create a new national political party. There have been several serious attempts over the last century. All of them have failed except in the case of regional parties with a geographically concentrated voter base like the Scottish National Party. The most recent attempt to break the mould was by Reform UK, a party led by Nigel Farage, which is the successor to the UK Independence Party and the Brexit Party. In the general election of July 2024, it won 14.29 per cent of the popular vote, 2 per cent more than the Liberal Democrats, but they won only five of the 650 seats compared with 64 for the Liberal Democrats. In England, which accounts for 83 per cent of the UK electorate, political activists have to operate within one or other of the existing national parties. Within each party, the fringes have to take over the centre if they want a voice in Parliament. Indeed, Nigel Farage has made no secret of his plan to take over the Conservative Party as Stephen Harper did in somewhat similar circumstances in Canada in 2003. With very small membership rolls dominated by activists, it is relatively easy to take over a political party from the fringes. The Labour Party was colonised, after losing power in 2010, by Momentum, a hard-left alliance that took over a large number of constituency associations. After 2017, Conservative constituency associations were gradually occupied by powerful Europhobic groups whose natural home would have been the UK Independence Party or the Brexit Party in a more diverse political system.

The effect of this polarisation on democratic politics is potentially very serious. The first task of any democracy is to accommodate differences of opinion and interest in the population, so that people can live together in a single political community without the systematic application of coercion. Political parties have had a major role in this process. They operate in a political marketplace. To command a parliamentary majority, they have to appeal to a much broader range of opinion than their own members. Their whole object is to produce a slate of policies that few people would endorse in its entirety but that the broadest possible range of people can live with. This has made them powerful engines of national compromise. The takeover of both major national parties by their fringes risks destroying the political market. It polarised party politics and limited the choices available to voters at general elections. The process was dramatically illustrated in the general election of December 2019, when the electorate was faced with a choice between a Labour Party led by Jeremy Corbyn with an extreme left-wing programme, and a Conservative Party led by an adventurer, Boris Johnson, with a programme of uncompromising anti-Europeanism. As for the Liberal Democrats, they have never had a chance of achieving power save perhaps in alliance with one or other of the two great Molochs of British politics.

The mechanics of democracy are different in other Western democracies, but the underlying problems are very similar. In the United States, the takeover of the Republican Party by activists has produced Donald Trump. In the Democratic Party, it had the ironic consequence in 2020 of enabling Joe Biden to stand as the party's candidate in spite of his limited basis of support, because the alternative would probably be a takeover by the party's radical left. In the French presidential election of 2017 the successful candidate, Emmanuel Macron, was preferred by less than a quarter of the electorate in the first round. A shift of just 3 per cent of the votes would have resulted in a run-off between the intransigent right of Marine Le Pen and the intransigent left of Jean-Luc Mélenchon. There is currently a serious possibility that exactly this will happen in the next presidential election, in 2027. The French legislative elections of July 2024 resulted in a legislative assembly polarised between a left block led by Mélanchon and a right block led by Le Pen, with the centre much diminished and incapable of forming a majority.

The Brexit referendum is a classic demonstration of the problems of polarisation. It divided the British electorate, 52 per cent voting to leave and 48 per cent to remain. It was intended to boost the Conservative Party by laying to rest the issue that had divided it for a generation. In fact, it destroyed it. It foisted on Parliament and on the parliamentary party a policy that MPs felt bound to adopt but in which most of them had little faith. They suppressed their doubts while they could. But they could not suppress them indefinitely, because our departure from the European Union left a major controversial issue unresolved on which the vote gave no guidance: what was to be Britain's social and economic model to replace the highly regulated and protectionist model represented by the EU? Brexit might have worked if we had become a low-tax, low-regulation economy (a model commonly referred to as 'Singapore on Thames'). That might have restored our historic rate of growth and enabled us effectively to compete against the enormous market power of the European Community next door. The trouble is that there is no appetite for such a thing in the electorate at large. The British are not small-state enthusiasts. They have the same aspiration for high regulation and expensive levels of public service as the rest of Europe. MPs, except for some zealots, know that Singapore-on-Thames is not going to be a ticket to re-election. But that is not accepted by a minority within the Parliamentary Conservative Party or the great majority of the Conservative Party at grassroots level. The result was a schism within the party.

The issue has not merely divided the Conservative Party on relations with Europe, an issue of critical importance to Britain's future. It has summoned up the Conservative Party's inner demons and delivered it into the hands of its snarling fringe. The fringe has generated fresh divisions on other, unrelated issues. It was these members who destroyed the government of Theresa May in collaboration with an opportunistic Labour Party, and enabled Boris Johnson and then Liz Truss to climb to power. A significant turning point came in November 2019, when twenty-one Conservative MPs who had resisted Johnson's hard line on Europe were purged from the party. The twenty-one included the leading members of the party's liberal wing, many of whom had been ministers in successive Conservative governments. The parliamentary whip was withdrawn from them and they were prevented from standing as Conservatives in the general election of December 2019. Those of them who tried to stand as independents were all defeated by official candidates. Those members of the parliamentary party who sympathised with the twenty-one purged members saved their seats by lying low. But they were bereft of influence.

With only a handful of generally short-lived exceptions, the Cabinet was thenceforth composed entirely of pro-Brexit Johnson loyalists. The impact of these events was hardened by the hubris that followed Conservative victory in the general election of December 2019. They obtained an absolute majority of 80 seats in the House of Commons, but never understood what had led to this result. The victory was attributed to Boris Johnson, especially by Johnson himself, although the extraordinary features of the moment and the deficiencies of Jeremy Corbyn had at least as much to do with it. The scale of the victory persuaded the party and its leader that they had found a new political base that made it unnecessary to appeal to a wider range of voters or to worry too much about competition from other political parties.

The purge of November 2019 and the general election of December 2019 were mortal blows to liberal conservatism. The grassroots members came out in great numbers to 'get Brexit done'. They have been disappointed by the result, which most of them attribute to the government's failure to grasp the benefits of Brexit and not to the fact that there are no such benefits and never were. As a result, they moved further to the extremes and supported fringe parties who really believe in this fantasy, leaving the Conservatives shorn of support on both left and right. Politics, like nature, abhors a vacuum. The result has been that a reformed Labour Party has moved into the centre ground where the Conservatives' main strength had traditionally been found. In the general election of July 2024, Labour won 411 seats, and the Conservatives were left with just 121 seats, less than a fifth of the House of Commons. In a century from now, Boris Johnson may turn out to have destroyed the Conservative Party as surely as David Lloyd George destroyed the Liberal Party in the decade after the First World War.

Two and a half millennia ago, Aristotle regarded democracy as an inherently unstable form of government because it was vulnerable to demagogues like these. The genius of modern Western representative democracy has been to defy that prediction for some two centuries. But how much longer will that continue if active politics are left to the fringes of established political parties? On critical issues, the political culture of Western democracies has lost the capacity to identify common premises, common bonds and common priorities that stand above our differences. This is contributing to the growing tendency on the part of the public to reject politics and the whole class of politicians. These divisions are damaging for a number of other reasons, but perhaps the most serious of them is that they correspond to major issues between generations. Younger people have often been more radical in their approach to politics than their elders. But the range and intensity of the difference between current generations is greater today than it has ever been. In Britain, Brexit was largely the work of an older generation of voters moved at least in part by nostalgia for a supposedly more harmonious past. For younger voters, Europe offered wider job opportunities and an internationalist ideology and culture that they found attractive. Climate change is a major issue for younger voters, but less so for older people who will be dead before the worst of it strikes. Restrictions on housebuilding have boosted the asset value of older home-owners while making it all but impossible for young families to get onto the property ladder in much of the country. The triple-lock system protects pensioners at the expense of younger taxpayers. The old had the benefit of free university education in their time, but the current generation of students have to fund their own tuition fees and commonly leave university with £50,000 or more of debt, which operates like a heavy graduate tax. The Conservative

Party has become essentially a party of the over-sixty-fives, its policies largely geared to maintaining their allegiance. The traditional assumption that people become more conservative as they grow older may be waning today. But for many younger voters, the blocking power of their elders is still generating a disillusionment with electoral democracy and a preference for disruptive direct action. These are symptoms of a dysfunctional community. If they persist, the probable outcome will be mounting internal violence, and ultimately some form of autocratic government. In the United States, where a similar chasm has opened up between the generations, this is already happening.

In Britain, there have been predictable calls for a written constitution. Yet I doubt whether the problems of Western democracies are capable of being resolved by formal legal or constitutional change. Even the most elaborate and law-based constitutional codes are soon overlaid by a body of practice and tradition, which is necessary to make them work. They depend for their effective operation on political conventions. Political conventions are rules of practice that are not legally enforceable but are observed because the political cost of ignoring them would be too high. That in turn requires a cross-party consensus which regards the effective operation of the political system as more important than success on any particular issue. Where democracies fail, it is usually the conventions that fail, not the law. The United States has one of the most formal and law-based constitutions in the world, while we have a constitution that is informal and political. Yet the two democracies in which the conventions of politics have most obviously broken down in the past decade are Britain and the United States. Donald Trump subverted the United States constitution by riding roughshod over its conventions without actually breaking any laws until the very end. The world is full of countries with impeccable constitutions and courts to enforce them, which have been subverted perfectly legally by governments. The democratic label remains on the bottle but the substance has been poured out of it by governments, often with public support.

The safeguards that ought to prevent this from happening are essentially cultural. They depend mainly on three things. Firstly, they depend on the capacity of representative institutions to dilute the impact of popular impatience and influential zealots, and to perform their traditional role of accommodating division and mediating dissent. Secondly, they depend on respect for conventional limits on the use of political power. Thirdly, they depend on active citizenship, by which I mean a willingness of people to participate in the political process at however humble a level and to do so in what they conceive to be in the public interest and not just in their own. This is an ideal. No society has ever perfectly attained it, and I am not so naïve as to think that they ever will. But they can get close enough for their politics to work.

After reading the gloomy thoughts which I have offered you up to now, you might be surprised to know that I am not entirely without hope. The British state, like other Western democracies, faces very serious challenges. Pressure for a more authoritarian model of democracy will intensify in the coming years. In important areas of our national life, these pressures will probably prevail over the liberal instincts that were taken for granted a generation ago. I do not welcome this prospect. But I think that the cultural and institutional foundations of our democracy will probably survive.

Let us look first at the capacity of Britain's representative institutions to perform their traditional role of accommodating division and dissent. This depends on a restoration of our broken political market. I think that this is already happening. Political parties exist to win power. To do that, they will sooner or later have to appeal for support well beyond their political base. But once they have got power, they have a tendency to turn inwards and to become increasingly preoccupied with the political prejudices of their most committed supporters. The cure for this endemic disease of political parties is a catastrophic electoral defeat followed by a long period in opposition. The usual response of political parties to defeat at the polls is to persuade themselves that they did not press their ideological convictions far enough. It usually takes at least two defeats to persuade them to adjust their offering to reflect political sentiment beyond their base. After Labour's defeat by Margaret Thatcher's Conservatives in the general election of 1979, the party was colonised at constituency level by a network of left-wing fringe groups called Militant Tendency. As a result, they went down to an even worse defeat in 1983. It was Labour's much-underrated leader Neil Kinnock who laid the groundwork for its eventual return to power by purging them from its list of approved candidates. Tony Blair completed the process by junking neo-Marxist policies like large-scale nationalisation in order the broaden the party's electoral base. The current leader of the Labour Party, Sir Keir Starmer, has done the same. After two successive defeats in 2015 and 2019, Starmer has displaced Jeremy Corbyn and skilfully used his majority on the Party's National Executive Committee to purge Momentum's supporters and return his party to its traditional left-of-centre position. He has been rewarded with a large parliamentary majority comparable to Tony Blair's majority of 1997, and a return of his party to government. This will be more difficult for the Conservatives to do. They will probably respond to the defeat in July 2024 by doubling down on their more extreme policies. That will keep them out of power for a decade or more. But eventually they will return to something like the centrist position that has made them such a successful party in the past. It is likely that Europe will be the critical test. A Labour government will move much closer to Europe and in the longer term a chastened Conservative Party will accept that.

Let us turn to the second item in my grounds for optimism, a respect for conventional limits on the use of political power. Like Trump in 2016, the Johnson government came to power in July 2019 with the classic trope of populist governments, namely that established institutions were conspiring to obstruct the popular will embodied in its own agenda. Johnson and his allies had a hit list of institutions that were liable to get in the way of the new government's ambitions: Parliament, the civil service, the courts and the BBC were all accused of obstructing the Brexit revolution. His principal adviser, Dominic Cummings, is said to have dismissed the House of Commons as 'pond life'. Johnson tried to silence Parliament by proroguing it at a critical point in the process of leaving the European Union. He sacked an unprecedented five departmental permanent secretaries and replaced the Cabinet Secretary with a relatively inexperienced official who was expected to be more malleable. He nominated his allies to the Board of the BBC. He promised to curb the power of the courts and for a time seriously considered abolishing the Supreme Court. Johnson's own conduct showed a cavalier disregard for basic standards of decency and political integrity, which had previously been an important part of the Conservative brand. This proved to be his undoing. His lies came back to haunt him when current and retired civil servants disclosed them. His nominee for chairman of the BBC was ousted on account of undisclosed conflicts of interest. Proposals to abolish the Supreme Court were stifled by the Justice Secretary and ultimately came to nothing. Finally, in July 2022, more than fifty members of his ministerial team resigned from his government on account of his mendacity.

It proved impossible to find enough people in his parliamentary party willing to replace them while he remained in power. The system spat him out. It was a remarkable and reassuring moment.

Much of Boris Johnson's agenda depended on the exercise of quasi-presidential powers by the prime minister. Indeed, in his final days in power, Johnson made an overt claim to presidential status. He claimed that the general election of December 2019 had conferred on him a personal mandate from the electorate that made it unconstitutional to evict him. Events proved him wrong. The electoral mandate belonged to his MPs, a large majority of whom refused to support him any longer. The process was repeated with Liz Truss, who was an honourable woman but lacked the basic standard of judgment and competence required for high office. She was imposed on her party by its grassroots membership and disposed of by the parliamentary party within six weeks. No democratic constitution can guarantee that only fit people will come to power. The real test of a constitution's resilience is its ability to get rid of them when their unfitness becomes apparent. By that test, the British constitution has done quite well.

Presidential constitutions like those of the United States or France have been much less efficient at disposing of unsatisfactory governments and objectionable ministers. It is, I think, worth lingering on the comparison with the United States. Boris Johnson was nothing like as destructive as Donald Trump. But the difference in their positions was institutional as well as personal. As the UK Supreme Court pointed out in the litigation over Brexit, a British government's sole mandate for power is the support of the House of Commons. Presidential systems are more vulnerable to the breakdown of political conventions than parliamentary systems. They confer a personal mandate on the president, who is practically immovable until the next election. They concentrate too much power in presidential hands, which is a serious problem if the individual is sufficiently determined to break the system. By comparison, parliamentary constitutions depend on a broader measure of cooperation within a larger political community. In the parliamentary world, conventions are usually more powerful and more difficult to discard. Trump was always able to find lieutenants to carry out his policies because senior civil servants are political appointments in the United States and ministers are not selected from the ranks of the elected legislature or answerable to it. Trump was able to pack the Supreme Court and other federal courts with ideological soulmates. None of these powers were available to Boris Johnson. He could have obtained them by legislation, but would probably have been unable to get the necessary bill through Parliament even with an eighty-seat majority. But perhaps the major difference between Britain and the United States is that in Britain it is the political parties that are polarised, whereas in the United States the move of the parties to the political fringes reflects the polarisation of the electorate at large.

Britain's constitution, much of which is common to Commonwealth countries, is imperfect. What constitution isn't? But it is worth reflecting on the combination of resilience and flexibility that has seen us through major crises in the past and will surely do so again. It has survived major changes that would have swept away more formal arrangements: the decline of the personal power of the monarch; the onset of mass democracy; the acquisition and then loss of a global empire; the existential crises of two world wars; and joining and then leaving the European Community. Few other national constitutions could have weathered these transformative events so well. France is on her fifth republic since the Revolution, with intervals for two Empires and a monarchy. Italy is on her fiftieth government since the war. We are more fortunate than we realise.

IV

A STATE OF FEAR*

Sir Robert Menzies was Australia's most distinguished twentieth-century premier. He was a liberal conservative, an individualist and a believer in the middle-class virtues of ambition, family loyalty and self-reliance. In all of these respects he was a man of his time, very much in the same mould as contemporary European statesmen such as Harold Macmillan in Britain and Konrad Adenauer in Germany. I was born the year before Menzies began his second premiership. In my adult lifetime, radical changes in our world have undermined many of the values that Menzies and his contemporaries held dear. The West's share of the world's resources and output, which Menzies took as a given, has been much reduced. Today, western economies are challenged by low-wage economies and the shortening of their technological lead. At the same time, there has been a dramatic rise in public demands on the state: as the provider of amenities; as a guarantor of minimum standards of economic security; and as the regulator of an ever-widening range of human activities. Coercion is the ordinary language of the state. When we transfer responsibility for our well-being from ourselves to the state, we invite a much more authoritarian style of government. In many ways the

* This is a slightly revised and updated version of a lecture delivered in October 2022 to the Robert Menzies Institute in Melbourne, Australia.

intellectual goalposts have shifted. It is more difficult to be a liberal conservative and an individualist in these conditions than it was in Menzies' day.

Perhaps the most striking manifestation of these change has been the response of most states to the pandemic. I am not going embark on a discussion of the merits of lockdowns as a response to Covid-19, although I am on record as doubting their effectiveness and objecting to their collateral consequences. I am concerned with a different question, namely what this episode in our history tells us about current attitudes to the state and to personal liberty. On that larger canvas, lockdowns are only the latest and most spectacular illustration of a wider tendency in our societies.

At the root of the political problems generated by the pandemic was the public's attitude to the state and to risk. People have a remarkable degree of confidence in the capacity of the state to contain risk and ward off misfortune. An earlier generation regarded natural catastrophes as only marginally amenable to state action. The Spanish flu pandemic of 1918–1921 is the event most closely comparable to the Covid-19 pandemic of 2020. It is estimated to have killed 200,000 people in the United Kingdom at a time when its population was about two-thirds of today's figure. Estimates of global mortality ranged from 20 to 100 million people at a time when the world's population was about a sixth of what it is now. Australia was largely protected from Spanish flu by distance and quarantine. In Europe, where it took a heavier toll, governments took no special steps to curtail its transmission, apart from isolating the infected and the sick, which had been the classic response to epidemics from time immemorial. No one criticised them for this. The related pathogens behind the Asiatic flu pandemic of 1957 and Hong Kong flu in 1968 had an infection rate roughly comparable to Covid-19, and a mortality rate that was somewhat lower. No special steps were taken to control transmission. Indeed, in the US and the UK a deliberate decision was made not to take such steps because of the disruptive effect that they would have had on the life of the nation. No one criticised this approach.

Covid-19 is a more infectious pathogen than Spanish flu, but it is significantly less mortal. It is also easier to deal with because it mainly affects those over sixty-five or suffering from one of a number of identifiable pre-existing clinical conditions, generally related to the respiratory system. A high proportion of people in those vulnerable categories are economically inactive. Governments might have worked with the natural instincts of humans for self-preservation, encouraging the vulnerable categories to shield themselves while the less vulnerable categories got on with their lives and engaged in the productive activities on which we all ultimately depend. Spanish flu was more difficult to deal with, because its most devastating impact was on healthy adults aged under fifty.

Yet in 2020, Britain, in common with Australia and almost all Western countries, ordered an indiscriminate lockdown of the whole population, healthy or sick, old or young, something that had never been done before in response to any disease anywhere. These measures enjoyed substantial public support. In Melbourne, lockdown was enforced with a brutality unequalled in liberal countries, but a Lowy Institute poll conducted in 2021 found that 84 per cent of Australians thought that their governments had handled it very well or fairly well. Australians thought even better of New Zealand's even tougher approach, with 91 per cent in favour. It is clear that in the intervening century between Covid-19 and Spanish flu, something radically changed in our collective outlook. Two things in particular have changed. One is that we now expect more of the state, and are less inclined to accept that there are limits to what it can or should do. The other is that we are no longer willing to accept risks that have always been inherent in life itself.

Human beings have lived with epidemic disease from the beginning of time. Covid-19 was a serious epidemic, but historically it was well within the range of health risks that are inseparable from ordinary existence, risks that human beings have always had to live with. In Europe, bubonic plague, smallpox, cholera and tuberculosis were all worse in their time. Worldwide, the list of comparable or worse epidemics is substantially longer, even if they did not happen to strike Europe or North America. Covid-19 is certainly within the broad range of diseases that we must expect to live with in future. The change is in ourselves, not in the nature or scale of the risks.

Epidemic disease is a particularly clear example of the kind of risks from which we now crave the protection of the state, although they are inherent in life itself. In modern conditions, risk aversion and the fear that goes with it are a standing invitation to authoritarian government. If we demand state protection from risks that are inherent in life itself, these measures will necessarily involve the suppression of some part of life itself. Legal regulation is designed to limit risk by limiting freedom. Governments do this to protect themselves from criticism. During the pandemic, regulations addressed the risk of infection by Covid because governments identified that as the thing they were most likely to be criticised for. Governments were willing to accept considerable collateral damage to mental health resulting from the lockdown and large increases in deaths from other causes such as cancer, ischaemic heart disease and dementia, because they knew that they were less likely to be criticised for those. They would not show up in TV screens, with pictures of long lines of ambulances waiting outside hospitals. They would not appear in daily casualty lists. They would show up only in obscure statistical tables published long after the event. But they are just as real.

In the first of my 2019 Reith Lectures, I drew attention to the implications of public aversion to risk for our relationship with the state. I referred to what I have called, then and since, the Hobbesian bargain. The seventeenth-century English political philosopher Thomas Hobbes argued that human beings surrendered their liberty completely, unconditionally and irrevocably to an absolute ruler in return for security. Hobbes was an apologist for absolute government. In his model of society, the state could do absolutely anything for the purpose of reducing the risks that threaten our well-being, other than deliberately kill us. Hobbes's state was an unpleasant thing, but he had, I think, grasped a profound truth. Most despotisms come into being not because a despot has seized power, but because people willingly surrender their freedoms in return for security. Our culture has always rejected Hobbes's model of society. Intellectually, it still does. But in recent years it has increasingly tended to act on it. The response to Covid-19 took that tendency a long way further. I could not have imagined in 2019 that my concerns would be so dramatically and so quickly vindicated.

Until March 2020, it was unthinkable that liberal democracies would confine healthy people in their homes indefinitely, with limited exceptions at the discretion of government ministers. It was unthinkable that a whole population would be subject to criminal penalties for associating with other human beings and answerable to the police for all the ordinary activities of daily life. When, in early February 2020, the European Centre for Disease Control published the pandemic plans of all twenty-eight then members of the EU, including the United Kingdom, not one of these plans envisaged a general lockdown. The two most influential plans were those prepared by the UK Department of Health and the Robert Koch

Institute, the official epidemiological institute of Germany. They came to remarkably similar conclusions. They did not propose measures to prevent the transmission of the disease. This was thought to be impossible, as indeed it has proved to be. Instead, they proposed to palliate its consequences. The great object should be to enable ordinary life to continue as far as possible. The two main lessons were, first, to avoid indiscriminate measures and concentrate state interventions on the vulnerable categories; and, secondly, to treat people as grown-ups, go with the grain of human nature and avoid coercion. The published minutes of SAGE, the committee of scientists advising the UK government, suggest that their advice was on the same lines right up to the announcement of the first lockdown. It is sometimes argued that these plans were irrelevant or inappropriate because they assumed that the pathogen behind a future pandemic would be a new variant of flu. But this is a red herring. The plans assumed a highly infectious pathogen that might be transmitted asymptomatically and might lead to upwards of 700,000 deaths in the United Kingdom alone. Those were all the characteristics that were needed to plan for Covid-19.

In Britain, the man mainly responsible for persuading the government to impose a lockdown was Professor Neil Ferguson, an epidemiological modeller based at Imperial College London. His work was influential both in the UK and elsewhere. In a press interview in February 2021, Professor Ferguson explained what had changed to justify a resort to lockdowns. It was the Chinese example. 'It's a communist one party state, we said. We couldn't get away with it in Europe, we thought … And then Italy did it. And we realised we could.' It is worth pausing to reflect on what this means. It means that because a lockdown of the entire population appeared to work in a country which was notoriously indifferent to individual rights and traditionally treats human beings as mere instruments of state policy, they could 'get away with' doing the same thing in Britain. Entirely absent from Professor Ferguson's analysis was any conception of the principled reasons why it had hitherto been unthinkable for Western countries to do such a thing. It was unthinkable because it was based on a conception of the state's relationship with its citizens that was morally repellent even if it worked.

It is not simply the assault on the concept of liberty that matters. It is the particular liberty that has been most obviously discarded, namely the liberty to associate with other human beings. Association with other human beings is not just an optional extra. It is fundamental to our humanity. Our emotional relationships, our mental well-being, our economic fortunes, our entire social existence is built on the ability of people to come together. This is why I regard lockdowns as a sustained attack on our humanity. Historically, the response to an epidemic like this would have been a matter for individuals to make their own risk assessments, in the light of their own vulnerability and those of the people around them. This was the policy pursued in Sweden, which avoided coercion. Sweden had a death toll broadly in line with the European average and considerably better than the UK's. None of the various attempts to argue that Sweden is in some relevant way different from the UK have been convincing. The imposition of a governmental decision applicable to the whole population irrespective of their individual situations is an extraordinary development in the history of our society and of other Western countries that have done the same thing.

The way that this one-size-fits-all approach has been justified adds to its totalitarian flavour. One argument that we heard, at least in the UK, was that uniform rules applied to people with different levels of vulnerability are necessary for the sake of social solidarity. There are two kinds of solidarity. One is the solidarity of mutual support. But this was a different kind of solidarity. It was the solidarity of intolerant conformism. It is irrational to treat everyone the same when the impact of the problem upon different sections of society is very different. The other argument was that it would be too difficult to enforce rules that differentiated between different people according to their degrees of vulnerability. In other words, the rules were couched in indiscriminate terms to make life easier for the police. When convenience of social control becomes itself an object of public policy, we are adopting part of the mentality of totalitarianism.

All of this marks a radical change in the relationship between the citizen and the state. The change is summed up in the first question that was asked of the UK prime minister when No. 10 press conferences were opened up to the public. 'Is it OK for me to hug my grand-daughter?' Something odd has happened to a society if people feel that they need to ask the prime minister if it is OK to hug their grand-daughter. I would sum up the change in this way. What was previously a right inherent in a free people has come to depend on government licence. We have come to regard the right to live normal lives as a gift of the state. It is an approach that treats all individuals as instruments of collective policy.

All of this was made possible by fear. Throughout history fear has been the principal instrument of the authoritarian state. Fear and insecurity were the basis on which Hobbes justified absolute government. That is what we witnessed in 2020 and 2021. A senior figure in the UK government told me during the early stages of the pandemic that in his view the liberal state was an unsuitable set-up for a situation like this. What was needed, he said, was something more 'Napoleonic'. That says it all. At least as serious as the implications for our relations with the state are the implications for our relations with each other. The use of political power as an instrument of mass coercion fuelled by public fear is corrosive. It is corrosive even, perhaps especially, when it enjoys majority support. For it tends to be accompanied, as it has been in Britain, by manipulative government propaganda and vociferous intolerance of the minority who disagree. Authoritarian governments fracture the societies in which they operate. The pandemic generated distrust, resentment and mutual hostility among citizens in most countries where lockdowns were imposed.

It is widely assumed that this is a phase that will pass when Covid-19 disappears (if it ever does). I am afraid that this is an illusion. We have turned a corner, and it will not be easy to go back. I say that for several reasons.

The first and most obvious reason is that governments rarely relinquish powers that they have once acquired. In Britain, wartime controls were kept in place for years after the end of the war. Food rationing was kept in place in the name of social solidarity until 1952, long after it had disappeared in Germany and in the European countries that Germany had overrun during the war. Regulations requiring people to carry identity cards, which had been introduced in 1940 to control spies and fifth columnists, remained in force for the convenience of the police until the mid-1950s. This was the social solidarity argument in action.

My second reason is that I see no reason why politicians should want or need to respect basic liberal values if the public is happy to dispense with them. Remarkably, an opinion poll taken in December 2023, more than two years after the last British lockdown had been lifted, suggested that a very substantial minority thought that it should still be in force. A high proportion of these were young people who had never been at significant risk of serious illness or death. There will be other pandemics, which will provoke the same public reaction. But public support for authoritarian measures is not simply a response to epidemic disease. It is a response to a much more general feeling of insecurity, combined with a profound faith in the ability of government to solve any problem with sufficient talent and money. This is a symptom of a more general appetite for authoritarian government, as the price for greater security.

It is accentuated by a growing feeling that strong governments are efficient while deliberative assemblies like Parliament are just a waste of time and a source of inefficiencies. Strongmen get things done. They do not waste time in argument or debate. Something of the flavour of this mentality can be seen in Australia in the decision of the then federal prime minister to assume the powers of five different ministries in addition to those of his own office. He must have believed that a single all-powerful figure was needed. The same thinking must have been at least in some degree responsible for the suspension of Parliament in Victoria. Discussion and debate were thought to get in the way of the effective exercise of power. Historical experience should warn us that this veneration of the strongman is usually wrong. Autocratic government is usually bad government. You might say: well, if the public is happy, isn't that democracy in action? I answer that that is how democracies destroy themselves. Democracies are systems of collective self-government. There is a point beyond which the systematic application of mass coercion is no longer consistent with any notion of collective self-government. The qualified house imprisonment of the entire population passed that point by a distance.

My final reason for believing that we have turned a corner on liberal democracy is perhaps the most fundamental. Aristotle objected to democracy because it was too easily transformed into despotism by the natural tendency of people to fall for an appealing tyrant. This is why some form of authoritarian government has always been the default position of mankind. Nevertheless, over two centuries most Western democracies have resisted this tendency and have avoided the disintegration that Aristotle regarded as its natural end. What has enabled them to do this is a shared political culture. Governments have immense powers, not just in the field of public health but generally. These powers have existed for many years. Their existence has been tolerable in a liberal democracy only because of a culture of restraint, a sense of proportion and a respect for our humanity, which made it unthinkable that they should be used in a despotic manner. It has only ever been culture and convention which prevented governments from adopting a totalitarian model. But culture and convention are fragile. They take years to form but can be destroyed very quickly. Once you discard them, there is no barrier left. The spell is broken. If something is unthinkable until someone in authority thinks of it, the psychological barriers that were once our only protection against despotism have vanished. There is no inevitability about the future course of any historical trend. But the changes in our political culture seem to me to reflect a profound change in the public mood, which has been many years in the making and may be many years in the unmaking. We are entering a Hobbesian world, the enormity of which has not yet dawned on our people.

V

HONG KONG: A MODERN TRAGEDY*

Hong Kong is one of the string of world cities created by Britain in the two centuries of its imperial history: Hong Kong, Mumbai, Singapore, Sydney. A British Crown colony founded on an uninhabited island off the Chinese coast in 1842, it has been a Special Administrative Region of China since it was handed back to them in 1997. Yet it has little in common with the nation to which it now belongs apart from ethnicity. It has a capitalist economy, and is lightly taxed and regulated. Its GDP per capita is among the highest in the world. It has its own currency, linked to the US dollar. Its institutions still bear the imprint of a century and a half of European administration. Its public affairs are conducted mainly in English. English was the medium of instruction in Hong Kong's schools and universities until 1997, and still is in the most prestigious institutions. Many students complete their education in the United States, Britain or Canada. Hong Kongers have an international outlook, sharing the aspirations and liberal instincts of their contemporaries in Europe and North America. The English common law has

* I was a Non-Permanent Judge of Hong Kong's Court of Final Appeal from 2019 until I resigned in June 2024. I had previously defended the Court, but recent developments persuaded me that it was no longer feasible for me to continue. A summary of my reasons appeared in the Financial Times on 11 June 2024. This chapter gives a fuller account.

its own liberal bias and remains the basis of Hong Kong's law.

To understand Hong Kong's current problems, it is necessary to go back into the history of this remarkable place. In spite of its many cultural and economic links with Britain and the West, the territory's modern history has been dominated by the enormous presence of China. During the twentieth century the population of Hong Kong rose rapidly, as it became a magnet for migrants fleeing from the civil wars of China before the Second World War and from communism afterwards. From some 850,000 inhabitants in 1931 it has grown to about 7.5 million today. The great majority of these people are either refugees or descended from refugees from China. China had significant influence among the territory's population even while it was under British rule. Before the war, the Kuomintang (the Nationalist Party of China) had friends and agents everywhere in the colony. After it, the communist government in Beijing was able to apply pressure through local communist parties, trades unions and the state news agency Xinhua. The Hong Kong office of the Bank of China served informally as China's diplomatic agency in the territory. In 1967 there were serious riots in the city inspired by the Cultural Revolution on the mainland. But the main source of China's influence was that it was always obvious that it would in due course recover the colony. Independence was not an option. Since the 1920s, China has declined to recognise the 'unequal treaties' by which Hong Kong was ceded to Britain. The territory was always indefensible. As Deng Xiaoping once told Mrs Thatcher, China could take possession of Hong Kong in an afternoon if they chose to. In practice, however, the most likely date for the return of Hong Kong to China was always 1997. Hong Kong Island was a British freehold, but it was not viable without the New Territories, an area of 368 square miles on the mainland and offshore islands from which the colony derived almost all of its water and electricity-generating capacity and where much of the population lived. The New Territories were held on a 99-year lease expiring on 30 June 1997.

The origins of Hong Kong's problems lie in the period immediately after the Second World War. In the 1950s and 1960s Britain's colonies were given a large measure of self-government, with directly elected local legislatures, but this policy was not followed in Hong Kong. The main reason was concern that any significant constitutional change might provoke a hostile reaction from Beijing. It was unclear how a democratic legislature in Hong Kong would behave. Given the large number of political refugees in the colony, it might become a platform for opposition to China or for Chinese-inspired opposition to the colonial government. A number of projects for partial democratisation had been mooted in the aftermath of Britain's reoccupation of Hong Kong in 1945 following Japan's wartime occupation. But in 1952, the Cabinet in London decided to drop all of them. The then colonial secretary informed Parliament that any substantial constitutional change would be 'inopportune'. It remained inopportune for the next thirty years. In hindsight, this was unfortunate. If democratic institutions had been firmly embedded in Hong Kong's system of government, they might well have survived the transfer of the territory to China in 1997. Instead, when the British came to negotiate Hong Kong's future the Chinese government, perhaps understandably, objected to attempts at the last minute to introduce a democratic system. They did not wish to see their authority limited in a way that the British had never been willing to accept during their own rule.

Negotiations with China opened in 1982. Once it became apparent that China was not prepared to extend Britain's tenure, the talks focused on trying to get the best deal for the population after the handover. With the deadline just fifteen years away, Britain had an exceptionally weak hand. Its only bargaining chip was the economic value of Hong Kong to China. At the time, Hong Kong was booming. It was China's most important economic outlet to the world, a major entrepôt for trade in physical goods. It was Asia's leading financial services hub and a significant source of investment capital. Its GDP was almost a fifth of China's. People and businesses had already begun to leave the territory for fear of what might follow after 1997. Hong Kong's value as an economic asset would be largely destroyed unless some measure of continuity could be negotiated. However, valuable as capitalist Hong Kong was to China, the recovery of its historic territory mattered more to China's leadership. The reality was that China could impose whatever solution it wanted, with or without Britain's agreement. In the circumstances, the Sino-British Joint Declaration, the treaty signed in Beijing in 1984, was as much as Britain could get, and more than many insiders had expected. China agreed to the principle of 'One Country – Two Systems'. Hong Kong would become a 'Special Administrative Region' under Chinese sovereignty, but with its own autonomous executive, legislative and judicial authorities responsible for everything except foreign affairs and defence. The current social, economic and legal systems would remain unchanged until at least 2047. Annexed to the Joint Declaration was a statement of Chinese policies regarding the territory, which included the principle of elections for the legislature. But nothing was said about the franchise and there was no commitment to universal suffrage. On the basis of the Joint Declaration, the Basic Law, a mini-constitution for Hong Kong, was drafted by a consultative committee comprising representatives of Hong Kong and the mainland. However, prominent pro-democracy figures on the committee were excluded by Beijing, and the result was only a very limited measure of democracy. The Basic Law was eventually promulgated in 1990, to take effect on the handover. Article 68 provided that the Legislative Council ('LegCo'), which approved Hong Kong's laws, would be constituted by election, but the electoral system was to be determined 'in accordance with the principle of gradual and orderly progress'. Universal suffrage was declared to be the 'ultimate aim', but no timetable was specified. Residents of Hong Kong were guaranteed a broad range of civil rights, including freedom of speech, conscience and assembly, and freedom of the press. But important legislative powers were reserved to the Beijing government. A political body in Beijing, the Standing Committee of the National People's Congress, was given the last word on the interpretation of the Basic Law.

At the time of the Sino-British Joint Declaration, LegCo consisted of nominees of the Governor and was dominated by government officials. Once the treaty had been signed, Britain embarked on a very cautious process of democratisation. The reason for the caution was that full democracy was resolutely opposed not only by Beijing but also by business interests in Hong Kong, which regarded it as destabilising. So a complex system was devised with an inbuilt anti-democratic bias. The main technique employed was the creation of 'functional' constituencies side by side with 'geographical' ones. Geographical constituencies represented the population at large. Functional constituencies represented business and the professions and were dominated by corporate voters. They elected councillors who were politically conservative and could generally be relied on to support the government. In 1991, the eighteen geographical constituencies were directly elected for first time by universal suffrage. By this time, the brutal suppression of the protests in Beijing's Tiananmen Square had created a powerful mood of suspicion and fear in the colony, especially among the large population of students. There had been massive demonstrations against China in Hong Kong itself. Pro-democracy groups won a landslide victory in the geographical constituencies, while pro-Beijing parties and groups representing business failed to win a single geographical seat. But the government was able to retain control and resist further democratisation because twenty-one of the sixty members were officials or government nominees, and another twenty-one represented the functional constituencies.

This awkward compromise was jettisoned by Chris Patten, the last British governor of Hong Kong, who was appointed in 1992. Patten determined to move immediately to a more democratic model and present China with a fait accompli. His reforms, which came into effect with the LegCo elections of 1995, removed the official and appointed element and broadened the electorate of the functional constituencies to comprise some 2.7 million voters. The result was that pro-democracy parties and their allies obtained a narrow majority in LegCo, including a third of the functional constituencies. Patten's reforms were popular in Hong Kong, but they brought him into direct conflict with the Chinese government and with most of the business community. He was supported by the Foreign Secretary, Douglas Hurd, himself a former career diplomat who had once served in the British embassy in Beijing. But senior China hands in the Foreign Office were appalled and said so. Beijing famously denounced Patten as the 'sinner of a thousand generations' and refused to recognise the new LegCo. It is at least arguable that Patten might have achieved more if he had been less ambitious and less confrontational. As it was, he achieved nothing. Beijing established a 'Provisional Legislative Council', comprising its own allies in Hong Kong, which sat in Shenzhen just across the border. The British declined to recognise this body, but after the handover, it moved to Hong Kong and replaced the elected LegCo of 1995. The new LegCo promptly abolished Patten's electoral reforms, restored the old-style functional constituencies and made a number of other changes that strengthened the pro-Beijing camp. The pro-democracy contingent in LegCo was sharply reduced in the elections which followed. These events ensured that the electoral system would be the main bone of contention in Hong Kong politics for years to come.

With LegCo largely neutered, opposition to the government took to the streets. The first Chief Executives were native Hong Kongers who had served in the colonial civil service or on the Governor's Executive Council before the handover. They tried to balance the conflicting demands of Beijing and the growing body of politically active Hong Kongers in conditions of increasing political tension. The first trial of strength concerned legislation about national security. The Basic Law required Hong Kong to enact a national security law criminalising treason, secession, sedition, subversion and ties with foreign political organisations. To comply with this requirement, the Hong Kong government introduced a home-grown National Security Bill into LegCo in February 2003. On 1 July 2003, the largest demonstration in the territory's history brought an estimated half a million people onto the streets. The Chief Executive, C. H. Tung, had close relations with Beijing, but was concerned about the risk of public unrest. The draft law was dropped. For the next fifteen years there were various proposals for introducing more democracy, all of which foundered as each project was rejected as too bold by China and too timid by Hong Kong's pro-democracy politicians. There were large-scale demonstrations in the streets; opinion polls disclosed high levels of hostility to mainland China; and an incipient movement pressed for independence from China, which alarmed Beijing, although it never acquired much traction.

Between March 2019 and January 2020 the tensions came to a head in a series of demonstrations and strikes that brought central Hong Kong to a standstill. The movement was nominally directed against a proposed extradition law, which would have enabled alleged offenders to be extradited to any territory with no extradition treaty with Hong Kong, including China. But the background was a more general dissatisfaction with slow progress towards full democracy, especially among students. The demonstrations became violent. The LegCo building was attacked, fires were lit, and there were violent clashes with the police. Many people were arrested and convicted of a variety of public order offences. Several people were killed. In October 2019, the Chief Executive, Carrie Lam, withdrew the draft extradition law. But the protests continued in support of an enquiry into allegations of police brutality and demands for Lam's resignation, with the demonstrators calling for universal suffrage for all LegCo seats. In November 2019, in the midst of these events, local government elections returned large pro-democratic majorities. Pro-Beijing groups suffered their biggest electoral reverse since the handover.

In the aftermath of the local government elections, pro-democracy politicians began to organise for the next elections to LegCo, which were due in September 2020. They arranged unofficial primaries to select a common list of pro-democracy candidates. At the time, LegCo had seventy members, equally divided between geographical and functional constituencies. The plan was to campaign in both categories for a majority that would demand universal suffrage and other concessions as a condition of approving the budget. The right of LegCo to withhold approval of the budget is enshrined in the Basic Law, which provides that if the Chief Executive fails to get the budget through twice, he must resign. It is one of the few ways in which LegCo can express no confidence in the government of Hong Kong. The campaign took off. Some 600,000 people voted in the primaries.

Beijing took fright. The arrival of Xi Jinping as paramount leader in 2012 had brought with it a more authoritarian tone in Chinese policy towards dissent in both Hong Kong and the mainland. Agitation by marginal groups proposing secession from China angered the central government, with Beijing particularly concerned about the prospect of a pro-democratic majority in LegCo that might open a Pandora's box of unwelcome initiatives. In May 2020 Beijing announced that since Hong Kong had failed to enact a home-grown national security law as required by the Basic Law it would impose one of its own. The National Security Law was passed by the Chinese legislature on 30 June, and came into force in Hong Kong on 1 July. It proved to be a great deal more draconian than the draft law whose enactment had been frustrated by the protests of 2003. It created four offences: planning, participating in or 'advocating' the secession of Hong Kong from China; committing or advocating subversion, defined as overthrowing or advocating the overthrow of the government of China or any interference with the functions of the government of Hong Kong; terrorist activities, defined as using violence or 'other dangerous activities endangering security' for any political purpose; and colluding with any foreign entity or receiving funding or support from a foreign enemy for the purpose of (among other things) disrupting the formulation or implementation of the laws of Hong Kong, imposing external sanctions on Hong Kong or provoking 'hatred' of the governments of China or Hong Kong. 'Principal offenders' were liable to stiff sentences ranging from ten years to life imprisonment. The law provided for the establishment in Hong Kong of an 'Office for Safeguarding the National Security of the Central People's Government'.

Its purpose would be to collect intelligence and to 'oversee, guide and coordinate' the national security functions of the Hong Kong authorities. There was, however, an important qualification to this catalogue of measures. Article 4 expressly preserved 'the rights and freedoms, including the freedoms of speech, of the press, of publication, of association, of assembly, of procession and of demonstration, which the residents of the Region enjoy under the Basic Law of the Hong Kong Special Administrative Region and the provisions of the International Covenant on Civil and Political Rights and the International Covenant on Economic, Social and Cultural Rights as applied to Hong Kong.'

The LegCo elections of September 2020 never took place. They were postponed by the Chief Executive under emergency powers, ostensibly because of the Covid-19 pandemic. By the time they were finally held, in December 2021, the electoral system had changed beyond recognition. LegCo was overhauled to make a pro-democracy majority impossible. The number of seats rose from seventy to ninety, and the number of directly elected geographical constituencies was reduced from thirty-five to twenty. All candidates were to be pre-vetted by a committee of government officials so as to exclude those who were not 'patriots' by Beijing's definition. At the same time the rules for interpreting the Basic Law were changed by statute. The Basic Law had always required public officials (including judges) to swear to uphold its provisions. This was henceforth to be interpreted as ruling out any attempt to 'indiscriminately' object to a government motion in LegCo with a view to threatening the government or forcing the Chief Executive to step down. Any attempt to organise an unofficial referendum so as to 'confront' the government was banned.

At this point, it is necessary to introduce the judiciary who would be called on to apply the new laws. Hong Kong has a developed legal culture with high ethical standards for both bench and bar. It maintains close relations with England where many Hong Kong lawyers received their legal education and training. The handover to China involved only one significant change to the judiciary. The Judicial Committee of the Privy Council, which had previously served as the colony's top court, was replaced with a new Court of Final Appeal, but the Basic Law allowed the recruitment of judges from other common-law jurisdictions. Shortly after the handover, the British government agreed with the then Chief Justice of Hong Kong to make available two serving judges from the top British court (then the Appellate Committee of the House of Lords) to sit part-time in Hong Kong as 'Non-Permanent Judges' of the new Court of Final Appeal. A number of retired judges were recruited to the Court, including British former law lords and leading judicial figures from Australia and Canada. The Court of Final Appeal has four Permanent Judges, including the Chief Justice. They sit in panels of five, with one Non-Permanent Judge assigned to join them for each appeal. The practice has been for each overseas Non-Permanent Judge to sit at roughly fifteen-month intervals for a month at a time. The overseas Non-Permanent Judges have an important symbolic role. Their presence is intended to reassure business interests that the basic structures and principles of the common law would remain intact, and that the rule of law would remain at the heart of the legal system. They have been described as 'canaries in the mine'.

The National Security Law impacted the independence of the judiciary at several points. In the first place, cases under the new law could be heard only by judges designated by the Chief Executive. This power is not as significant as it sounds. The less important cases are heard by district judges sitting without a jury. They have limited sentencing powers.

There are forty-three of them, and only about half a dozen are known to have been designated. So in their case, the Chief Executive has a real choice. In the High Court, which hears the more important cases, the Chief Executive does not. Until recently, there were only eleven criminal judges in the High Court and all or nearly all of them had to be designated in order to cope with the volume of business. The Chief Executive does not assign designated judges to particular cases. That is done by the Court itself. Carrie Lam, who was Chief Executive when the National Security Law was imposed, was in principle willing to designate overseas Non-Permanent Judges to hear national security cases. The current Chief Executive, John Lee, a former police officer, is not. The few national security cases that have reached the Court of Final Appeal (so far only on ancillary or procedural points) have been heard with one of the handful of Non-Permanent Judges permanently resident in Hong Kong. The second change was that although the High Court normally sits on criminal cases with a jury, the Secretary for Justice, a government minister, was given power to direct that national security cases be heard without a jury. This power is invariably exercised. The practice has been for the High Court to sit on national security cases in panels of three without a jury. It is difficult to say what impact this has had on the outcome of these cases, but trial by judges alone does at least mean that the reasons for their decisions are known and open to scrutiny not only by the appeal courts but by the world. Finally, and perhaps most significantly, the ultimate power to interpret the National Security Law is vested in the Standing Committee of the National People's Congress. In theory this would allow the Chinese government to interfere at will with the law declared by Hong Kong's courts. Whether this would be a problem in practice would depend on how ruthless they chose to be in exercising this right. Putting it at its lowest, the power of designation and the vesting of a right of interpretation in the Standing Committee suggest a measure of distrust in the judiciary on the part of Beijing.

When the National Security Law was introduced, there were already perfectly adequate laws on the Hong Kong statute book dealing with outbreaks of political violence such as the riots of 2019. Violence of that kind would have been criminal in any country in the world including the UK. It was therefore unclear exactly what object Beijing wished to achieve by the new law. One obvious purpose was to fill the gap left by the inability of successive Hong Kong governments to pass a national security law of their own as required by the Basic Law. Another was an emphatic assertion of the unity of China (including Hong Kong and Taiwan) and the authority of the state. However, it soon became clear that the Chinese government was set on using the new law to achieve the systematic suppression not just of democracy but of public advocacy of democracy and, more generally, of political opposition of any kind. Hong Kong has never been a democracy, but the rule of law can flourish without democracy, as it traditionally had done in Hong Kong. It is more difficult for the rule of law to flourish without some basic liberties including freedom of speech, conscience and opinion. In practice, societies that set about suppressing these things almost always have to confer a large measure of arbitrary discretion on officials and police officers. This would severely test the judges. They would have to give a precise interpretation of vague expressions such as 'hatred' of China, 'interference' with the functions of the government, or 'collusion' with foreign entities. They would also have to decide how the National Security Law was to be read together with the saving for civil rights in Article 4. Most of the new offences created by the National Security Law have their equivalents in the legislation of other countries, including many liberal democracies. A great deal depends on how such provisions are used and where the threshold of liability is placed. In private conversations at the time, judges appeared confused and apprehensive, but basically optimistic. They reacted with some indignation to the suggestion that they would be influenced by political pressures in deciding cases. There were different views on how far they would or should be influenced by a fear that Beijing would exercise its right to 'interpret' the National Security Law. Most expected to apply the law like any other statute, irrespective of what they thought might ultimately emerge from Beijing. These attitudes were to come under growing pressure over the following years.

Early police operations were directed by the Beijing National Security Office, a police intelligence organisation and political directorate whose officials arrived in Hong Kong from the mainland a week after the new law came into force. Five weeks later, on 10 August 2020, there was a heavy-handed raid by some 200 police on the offices of *Apple Daily*, the biggest Chinese-language newspaper in Hong Kong. *Apple Daily* had never supported the secession of Hong Kong from China, but it had for many years been a vocal supporter of the pro-democracy movement. In consequence the paper, and its proprietor and editor-in-chief Jimmy Lai, had been the target of persistent vituperation in the state media of the mainland and in the two Beijing-controlled Chinese-language papers in Hong Kong, *Wen Wei Po* and *Ta Kung Pao*. In the course of the raid Jimmy Lai was arrested along with his two sons, two senior executives of the paper and some reporters, a total of ten people. Lai was paraded through the streets in handcuffs. *Apple Daily* was subsequently closed down by the police under powers conferred by the National Security Law, without any judicial process. Beijing's Office of Hong Kong and Macao Affairs did not wait for the trial before issuing a statement applauding the arrests and calling for Jimmy Lai to be severely punished. Successive charges have been laid against Lai, designed to keep him indefinitely in prison in a manner reminiscent of the treatment of Khodorkovski and Navalny in Russia or Aung San Suu Kyi in Myanmar. The main charge against him is colluding with foreign powers, principally the United States, against the interests of China and Hong Kong. Jimmy Lai has never denied that he sought to persuade foreign powers to impose sanctions on Hong Kong in support of the pro-democracy movement, but he says that he did this before the National Security Law came into force, when it was entirely legal. The prosecution contends that the support of *Apple Daily* for democracy constituted sedition and was criminal even before the National Security Law. To this contention, Jimmy Lai's answer is the safeguards to freedom of the press in both the Basic Law and the National Security Law itself. Lai's trial did not open until the end of December 2023, three and a half years after his arrest. It is still not concluded as I write this in September 2024. In the meantime, he has been sentenced to two terms of twenty months imprisonment for participating in illegal assemblies. As these sentences were about to expire, a district judge convicted him of the fraudulent use of his own office space, on the surprising ground that the use of part of the premises by Lai's consultancy company in breach of a covenant in the lease was a criminal fraud. He was sentenced for this offence to five years and nine months imprisonment. It is impossible to believe that this would have happened to someone who was not in Beijing's gunsights.

Jimmy Lai is one of many people accused of speech crimes who have been charged under the colonial-era Sedition Ordinance, originally promulgated in 1938, later re-enacted in the Crimes Ordinance. The ordinance is drafted in extraordinarily broad terms. It criminalises any words uttered or acts done with the intention of raising 'discontent of disaffection' against the Crown or the government of Hong Kong. The status of this legislation is debatable. Until 2020, it had not been used since the communist-inspired riots of 1967. There is statutory protection in Hong Kong for freedom of expression and the right of protest, under the Hong Kong Bill of Rights, which gives effect to the International Convention on Civil and Political Rights. The Bill of Rights repeals any pre-existing legislation so far as it is inconsistent with its terms. The repeal provision was, however, ruled incompatible with the Basic Law by an 'interpretation' by the Standing Committee of the National People's Congress shortly before the handover. Hong Kong's Court of Appeal has taken a hard line on sedition under the Crimes Ordinance. In the first case to come before it, a democracy activist had been sentenced to twenty-one months in jail for using a loudhailer in the streets to shout 'Liberate Hong Kong' and various slogans abusing the police and the government. Dismissing his appeal, the Court held that freedom of speech could lawfully be restricted in the interests of national security and that it was irrelevant whether the defendant had any intention to incite violence.

Jimmy Lai's is the most high-profile national security case, but it is far from being the only one. According to figures released by the Hong Kong government in June 2024, 299 people have been arrested in what the government calls 'national security and related cases'. Of these, 59 per cent were subsequently charged. About a third of these were charged with 'endangering national security' through online posts or public statements. The conviction rate is almost 100 per cent.

The first target of prosecutions under the National Security Law and the Crimes Ordinance was the pro-democracy press. After the enforced closure of *Apple Daily*, in December 2021 there was a raid by more than 200 police on the offices of

Stand News, an online news outlet that had given sympathetic coverage of the pro-democracy movement. Seven journalists were arrested. The editor and his deputy were subsequently charged under the Crimes Ordinance with the publication of seditious material. *Stand News* ceased publication shortly after the raid. The two defendants were held on remand for nearly a year until they were granted bail at the opening of their trial in December 2022. The case is important because the prosecution was based entirely on the publication in the press of political opinions. Freedom of speech and of the press was the only issue. The prosecution case was based on the publication in 2020 and 2021 of seventeen articles none of which could reasonably be construed as calls to violence or rebellion. Most of them were interviews or profiles featuring prominent supporters of democracy in Hong Kong. The case was tried before District Judge Kwok Wai-Kin, who has distinguished himself for his zeal in sedition and national security cases. At one stage in 2021 the then Chief Justice had directed that politically controversial cases should not be listed before him because of his habit of delivering political speeches from the bench. On 29 August 2024, Judge Kwok convicted both defendants. He held that if the journalists' intention was to undermine the legitimacy of the authorities in Beijing or Hong Kong, it was irrelevant that there was no real risk to national security. The judge was dismissive of arguments based on proportionality or the Hong Kong Bill of Rights. Once the relevant intention had been proved, he held, that was the end of the matter. On that basis he found that eleven of the seventeen articles were seditious. This was because the articles publicised criticisms of the National Security Law or the sedition law, or the way that they had been enforced or the treatment of protesters by the police. In the judge's view these criticisms had 'no objective basis'. In some cases they were said to have been endorsed by the editors. The editor was sentenced to twenty-one months in jail, and his deputy to eleven months. 'They were not doing genuine journalistic work', said Judge Kwok in his sentencing remarks, 'but taking part in the so-called resistance against the government.' There could hardly be a clearer statement that the expression of opinions hostile to the government is now to be treated as criminal.

Cases like this had a chilling effect on other media outlets even before the verdict was announced. Some public discussion programmes have been taken off-air by Hong Kong's public service broadcaster, together with a number of political programmes including much of the output of the BBC World Service. Internet service providers in Hong Kong have blocked access to the websites of organisations critical of the government, such as the UK-based Hong Kong Watch. The foreign press is freely available in Hong Kong, but foreign journalists thought to be critical of the government have been refused visas or excluded on arrival. There has been a good deal of self-censorship. The *South China Morning Post*, for example, Hong Kong's leading English-language paper, has suppressed articles on alleged human rights breaches in Xinjiang in China. This became known only because it provoked the resignation of two reporters. There are thought to be many other such cases that have not seen the light of day. In late 2022, a survey suggested that 70 per cent of Hong Kong-based journalists censor their own work to stay out of trouble. The Foreign Correspondents' Club has released the results of a survey of its members, which suggests that two-thirds of foreign correspondents based in Hong Kong either avoid politically sensitive subjects or censor their own copy. These journalists will all have taken note of the verdict in the *Stand News* case. If freedom to criticise the law or the government is the hallmark of a free press, then that case marks the end of freedom of the press in Hong Kong.

After the press, the authorities turned on dissenting political groups. On 6 and 7 January 2021, fifty-five people involved in organising the unofficial primaries of 2020 were arrested. Forty-seven of them were subsequently charged with 'conspiracy to commit subversion', contrary to the National Security Law. They included distinguished academics, prominent journalists, local government councillors, trades unionists and former members of LegCo. Most of them have been held on remand in jail ever since. Most organisations campaigning for democracy or human rights were disbanded over the following months. They included student unions and the two largest trades unions in Hong Kong, the Professional Teachers Union and the Hong Kong Confederation of Trades Unions. Many of their leaders have been arrested or have fled. The most notable victim was the Hong Kong Alliance in Support of Democratic Movements in China. For many years, the Alliance had organised a silent vigil in Victoria Park to honour the dead of the Tiananmen Square protests. These assemblies were banned after 2020, ostensibly under social distancing regulations during the pandemic. But it became the practice for people spontaneously to show their support on the day by lighting candles or shining mobile phone torches in streets, homes or offices wherever they happened to be. Tiananmen Square is a hot issue in Hong Kong, and a matter of extreme sensitivity in Beijing, which regards any sympathy for the protesters as provoking hatred of China. Chow Hang-Tung, a barrister, became the convener of the Hong Kong Alliance in 2021, after the two previous convenors had been jailed. She has been the victim of a prolonged legal vendetta by the authorities. On 5 June 2021, she was arrested along with twenty-five other prominent members of the Alliance and participants in the vigils. Chow was charged with promoting an unlawful assembly but released on bail. She was rearrested on 30 June

2021, and eventually granted bail on her third application on 5 August 2021. Apparently as a result of the grant of bail, she was rearrested on 8 September 2021, together with five other people involved in the Alliance, but this time charged with 'incitement to subversion', an offence to which the highly restrictive bail provision of the National Security Law applied. The basis of this charge was the refusal of the Hong Kong Alliance to supply information to the police to establish whether the Alliance was an 'agent of foreign forces'. Chow Hang-Tung was refused bail. She has subsequently been convicted and imprisoned for a total of twenty-two months on two charges of unlawful assembly, one relating to the 2020 vigil and the other to the 2021 vigil. In May 2024, after her release, she was again arrested, this time for allegedly publishing seditious social media posts relating to the Tiananmen Square protests. She is currently due to be tried in the High Court, with two others, in May 2025. She will by then have spent most of the previous four years in jail, with the prospect of more years imprisonment ahead of her. Meanwhile, the Hong Kong Alliance had been struck off the companies register by order of the Chief Executive on the grounds that it was a subversive organisation.

These have been the most high-profile cases. However, the target list has been expanded to include many very minor actors accused of trivial acts of opposition to the government.

In July 2021, five members of the General Union of Hong Kong Speech Therapists were arrested and charged with sedition contrary to the Crimes Ordinance. The charges arose out of the publication of three cartoon books for children about a pack of wolves attacking a village occupied by a flock of sheep. The books contained no explicit political statements, but the foreword to one of them referred to the 2019 riots and the epilogue included a chronology of recent political events in Hong Kong. This led to the inference that the wolves were intended to represent China and the sheep the people of Hong Kong. The accused were refused bail, and held on remand for thirteen months, more than half of the two-year maximum sentence for this colonial-era offence. At their trial before a district judge in July 2022 their defence was based on the right of free speech under the Hong Kong Bill of Rights and Article 4 of the National Security Law. All of them were convicted. In his reasons, the judge held that criticism of the Chinese government was an implicit call for the secession of Hong Kong. Although at common law and under international jurisprudence on the International Covenant on Civil and Political Rights, the offence of sedition required proof of an intention to overthrow the state by violence, this was said to be unnecessary in Hong Kong. No regard was paid to Article 4. All five accused were sentenced to nineteen months imprisonment. In his sentencing remarks, the judge described the publications as an exercise in 'brainwashing' children.

Peaceful protests have habitually been treated as sedition and punished with imprisonment. Examples include a sixty-nine-year-old busker convicted for playing the melody of 'Glory to Hong Kong', which has come to be regarded as the anthem of pro-democracy protesters; a man who engaged in a one-man protest, parading in the street with a coffin covered in slogans protesting against the electoral system; a radio host arrested for inciting secession and hatred of China, by setting up and publicising a crowd-funding scheme to help young Hong Kongers to study at universities in Taiwan; a well-known singer convicted for singing songs whose lyrics were said to incite opposition to government policies on vaccination; and two women, the proprietors of a teashop, who were arrested and charged with sedition for online social media posts opposing the government's Covid vaccination drive. Attempts to raise funds for opposition causes have generally been met with accusations of money laundering. These are just some of the regular toll of arrests, remands and convictions of critics of China or the Hong Kong government. They range from student discussions in campus meetings to social media posts, vigils outside police stations, press articles, and so forth. These events are milestones on the road to totalitarianism in a territory once notable for its vibrant political diversity. They are difficult to reconcile with the rule of law. The National Security Law gives too much discretionary power to the police to detain citizens on political grounds and disables the judiciary from intervening to grant bail so that at least they remain at liberty until convicted by a court. So far, all of these cases have been dealt with by magistrates or district judges. None of the High Court trials have been concluded, except for the trial of the forty-seven democracy activists, to which I shall return. Neither the Court of Appeal nor the Court of Final Appeal has had to deal with a case about the ambit of the new offences.

In the face of hardening judicial attitudes, the defence of those accused in these cases faces a steep uphill battle. Their task is made more difficult by officially sponsored harassment of lawyers representing people accused of offences under the National Security Law or criticising the law or decisions made under it. The most notable cases are those of Paul Harris, the chairman of the Hong Kong Bar Association until January 2022 and Michael Vidler, the founder and senior partner of a firm of Hong Kong solicitors specialising in criminal defence and human rights. Paul Harris, a British subject, was a prominent critic of the National Security Law and the government's prosecution policy. He was the subject of strident criticism in a public statement issued on 25 April 2021 by the Beijing liaison office in Hong Kong after he had objected to the jailing of peaceful protesters and called for a change in the law. He was said in the statement to have 'backed up lawbreakers, slandered law enforcement agencies and put pressure on the judiciary.' It was also said that he was a member of the UK's Liberal Democrat party, serving its interests, and that since he could not be expected to comply with the principle of 'patriots administering Hong Kong', he should no longer be chairman of the Bar Association. In February 2022 Michael Vidler was criticised by a district judge for distributing cards explaining the legal rights of those participating in public protests and giving contact details of lawyers who could help them if they got into trouble. He was subsequently summoned to a police station and questioned, although not charged with any offence. Both men subsequently left Hong Kong, citing official harassment as the reason. The Georgetown Centre for Asian law has reported a small number of instances, which are difficult to verify, of pressure being brought on defendants to retain 'trusted' advocates and not prominent legal critics of the National Security Law. In December 2022, a Reuters special report based on some fifty interviews with lawyers, reported repeated harassment of lawyers specialising in human rights or regularly defending those on criminal charges and suggested that some eighty of them had felt obliged to leave Hong Kong.

This is the background to measures to restrict the appearance of non-resident British lawyers in the Hong Kong courts in national security cases. Leading counsel from Britain have always been admitted to the Hong Kong Bar for important cases, but Beijing believes that in politically sensitive cases British lawyers are subject to pressure from their own government to associate themselves with opposition to the National Security Law. Unfortunately, this feeling has sometimes been encouraged by ill-advised statements by some British ministers and politicians. In the autumn of 2022, shortly before the date originally fixed for the trial of Jimmy

Lai, his British counsel, Tim Owen KC, applied in the ordinary way to be admitted temporarily to the bar to conduct his defence. The government opposed his admission, arguing that the use of overseas counsel was inappropriate in cases involving national security. The High Court allowed his admission and their decision was affirmed on appeal. The decision was fiercely criticised by Beijing-controlled media and by prominent pro-Beijing politicians, including the former Chief Executive C.-Y. Leung, the vice-chairman of Beijing's advisory committee on Hong Kong. Their arguments open a window on Beijing's approach to Hong Kong's English common-law legal system with its embedded scheme of civil rights. Leung argued that Hong Kong should not follow 'internationally adopted judicial standards' in cases involving national security. Beijing-controlled papers suggested that Owen's participation in the trial would create a 'bias' in favour of 'Western viewpoints'. The reasoning of the Hong Kong courts in Tim Owen's case has been effectively reversed by the Standing Committee of the National People's Congress. Article 47 of the National Security Law empowers the Chief Executive to certify which cases are to be treated as national security cases. The Standing Committee 'interpreted' this as requiring the courts to obtain the Chief Executive's permission for the use of overseas counsel in national security cases. It is difficult to regard this as an interpretation or as anything other than a political decision. Rights of audience are properly a matter for the court, not the executive and certainly not for the prosecuting authorities when the application concerns the representation of the defence. The issue has now been dealt with by amending the relevant ordinances to exclude the use of non-resident counsel from national security cases without government permission. Neither the 'interpretations' of the Standing Committee nor the amendments to the ordinances are retrospective, but the government has excluded Tim Owen by the simple device of refusing him a visa to enter Hong Kong in spite of the decision of the courts that he is entitled to be admitted to the bar to defend Jimmy Lai. An attempt to obtain a judicial review of this decision failed on the ground that it was not reviewable. Perhaps the most significant lesson of this affair is that Hong Kong and the Beijing Liaison Office in Hong Kong are developing a siege mentality in response to overseas criticism of the National Security Law. There is an increasingly powerful tendency to insulate the criminal justice system from contagion by the more liberal tradition of the English common law. An unspoken but very obvious purpose of limiting defence representation to resident lawyers is to ensure that the defence is subject to more overt and effective pressure from the Hong Kong authorities.

This was the situation in May 2024 when the High Court handed down its judgment in the case of the forty-seven democracy activists. By the opening of the trial, thirty-one of the forty-seven had pleaded guilty. Of the sixteen who remained, fourteen were convicted of conspiring to commit subversion. They were convicted on the ground that the object of their campaign in the 2020 elections had been to obtain a majority in LegCo and use it for a purpose unacceptable to the government. The Basic Law expressly provides for LegCo to reject the government's budget and for the Chief Executive to resign if it does so twice. But, said the Court, this only means that they could reject it on some ground relating to the budget itself. The power could not be used 'indiscriminately' as a way of bringing pressure on the government to change its policies. Since their demands would certainly have been unacceptable to the Chief Executive, the Court said, the budget would have been rejected and the Chief Executive would have had to resign. This would have interfered with the performance of the Chief Executive's functions as head of

government, contrary to the National Security Law. Therefore, they concluded, putting the plan before the electorate
was a criminal conspiracy. In a remarkable twist of reasoning, the Court applied the statutory amendments that had
been introduced a year after the events in question to prevent
similar campaigns in future. The amendments were not
retrospective, but the judges held that they had been 'explan-
atory' of the previous law. In due course, the fourteen will be
sentenced, along with the thirty-one who pleaded guilty. The
minimum sentence prescribed by the National Security Law
is ten years' imprisonment. The maximum is life.

The decision is in my view legally indefensible. It may
yet be reversed on appeal, although the appeal process is
likely to take years and I would not bet on the outcome. The
problem, however, is not just the decision itself but what it
tells us about the judicial mood in Hong Kong. Judges are
of course constrained by the terms of the National Security
Law and the ordinance against sedition. They have to apply
the law, whether they like it or not. But in those areas that are
left to their judgment, they have almost invariably allowed
themselves to become the instruments of government policy.
Their interpretations of the National Security Law are even
more repressive than its language. Any sense of proportion
has been lost, as conduct that could not possibly endanger
the state, mostly trivial acts of protest and dissent, are treated
as if they were calls for rebellion. The important savings for
civil rights in the Basic Law and the National Security Law
are usually ignored. When they are considered at all, only
lip service is paid to them. In November 2023 the Court of
Appeal held that national security and public order were 'paramount' with the result that the savings for civil rights had no
application in sedition cases, even if there was no intention
to incite violence. The Court of Final Appeal refused leave
to appeal on this point. Those who are convicted, whether

under the sedition law or under the National Security Law, receive savage sentences. The sentencing remarks of some district judges read like political speeches. Those defendants who pleaded guilty in the case of the forty-seven democracy activists had presumably concluded that there was no hope of acquittal in this atmosphere. They have been proved right.

Hong Kong's judges are honourable men and women sharing all the liberal instincts of the common law. Yet they have lost sight of the traditional role of the common law of defending the liberty of the subject against the overreaching state. How has this happened? Critics of the Hong Kong judiciary, such as the lawmakers in Washington who are pressing for sanctions against them, tend to forget that Hong Kong's judges have to work in an impossible political environment created by China. The territory's autonomy has been severely restricted since 2020. Beijing has imposed the new law, remade statutory provisions by way of 'interpretation' and intervened to direct police operations in cases deemed by them to affect national security. I do not for a moment believe that the government secretly leans on judges to get the 'right' answers. The tragedy is that they do not need to. In high-profile cases, such as Jimmy Lai's and the case of the forty-seven democracy activists, Beijing's Office for Hong Kong and Macao Affairs has made it very clear what outcome is expected. Defendants are denounced in vituperative terms in the pages of *China Daily*, the mouthpiece of the central government, and in the two Beijing-controlled Chinese-language papers in Hong Kong. Hefty sentences are demanded. On the rare occasions when those accused are granted bail or acquitted, there is a chorus of outrage from the pro-Beijing press and the pro-Beijing caucus in LegCo. There is a constant drumbeat of calls for patriotism across the public service, including the judiciary. The pro-Beijing media and some LegCo members have demanded a government commission to monitor the conduct of judges. It takes considerable courage for a judge to swim against such a strong political tide. And to what end? Every judge knows that any decision that Beijing sees as undermining its campaign to suppress dissent will effectively be reversed by an 'interpretation' from the Standing Committee of the National People's Congress. If the Standing Committee was willing to intervene on an issue as marginal as the use of English barristers in national security trials, what might one expect of it if the judges were to reject as a matter of legal principle the totalitarian implications of some of Beijing's current policies? A wise local judge put his finger on the problem. We cannot conduct a continual guerrilla war against the Chinese state, he told me. Hong Kong is part of China. Beijing is here to stay and will not change its spots. Our roots are in China and here in Hong Kong, he went on. What have China's Western critics got to offer, apart from moral lectures and second passports? There is no obvious answer to that.

Where does this leave the overseas Non-Permanent Judges of the Court of Final Appeal? Unlike local judges they have somewhere else to go. Some have already gone. One of them, the former Chief Justice of New South Wales Jim Spigelman, resigned in protest shortly after the imposition of the National Security Law. In 2022, the British government terminated the arrangement under which serving British judges were available to sit in the Court of Final Appeal, which meant that the two Non-Permanent judges on the UK Supreme Court, Lord Reed and Lord Hodge, had to resign. Lord Reed issued a statement in which he declared that the Hong Kong courts were committed to the rule of law, but he supported the decision on the ground that British judges 'cannot continue to sit in Hong Kong without appearing to endorse an administration which has departed from values of political freedom, and freedom of expression'.

The position of other overseas judges of the Court of Final Appeal is more complex. They do not sit courtesy of the British government. In their capacity as Hong Kong judges they do not take their cue from the British or any other government. Unlike Lord Reed, I do not believe that the presence of British judges on the Court of Final Appeal is an endorsement of Hong Kong's government, but it is unquestionably an endorsement of its judiciary. There are two situations in which an overseas judge might think it right to resign. One is that they consider that the judiciary is no longer sufficiently committed to the rule of law. The other is that even if judges conscientiously apply the law, the substance of the law is too objectionable for them to want to be part of the system. The argument for staying is that although the overseas judges have no direct influence on the way that the National Security Law is applied (none of them is likely to be designated to hear national security cases), they may nevertheless enjoy some indirect influence. Neither China nor the local judiciary wants to see them go, because their participation is a badge of legal respectability. Even in a difficult situation, their presence may bolster the common-law tradition, encourage adherence to the rule of law and help to repair its recent deficiencies. They can still perform a useful service to the people of Hong Kong by sitting on cases about torts, contracts, less politically sensitive criminal cases, and so on. A number of judges and other lawyers in Hong Kong have suggested to me that the mass departure of overseas judges might even make matters worse.

It is a difficult balance on which Hong Kong's overseas judges can and do legitimately differ. Two more overseas judges, Lord Collins and myself, resigned early in June 2024 because of the political situation in Hong Kong. I can only speak for myself. The National Security Law is excessively broad and its definitions unduly vague. However, it could have been applied in a way which respected the basic civil rights embodied in the Basic Law and in the National Security Law itself. This has not happened. The discretions vested in the Hong Kong police and the arbitrary way in which the law has been applied by the executive are not consistent with the rule of law. The current political atmosphere makes it exceptionally difficult for judges to do their job independently of government policy. In areas of direct concern to the government, the rule of law is therefore seriously compromised. The result in Hong Kong has been a string of administrative and judicial decisions that are characteristic of totalitarian states like mainland China.

For the future, the prospect is bleak. Since 2020, the Hong Kong government has found it more difficult to recruit judges. Retired British judges have been unwilling to accept appointment as Non-Permanent Justices of the Court of Final Appeal. It has proved difficult to recruit judges to the High Court from the bar. This last problem has been met in part by promoting district judges, often those who have been designated to hear national security cases and have proved to be reliable. In March 2024, the Beijing-imposed National Security Law was superseded by a home-grown statute that reproduces everything in the 2020 law but with wider definitions, more extensive examples of seditious conduct, and more elaborate provisions for enforcement. For the mass of citizens, the place still feels free. But it is dangerous to disagree with the government if you value your career, and dangerous to disagree publicly if you value your liberty.

The rule of law is indivisible. If it is not respected across the board, it will sooner or later wither across the board. I remained on the Court of Final Appeal in the hope that the presence of overseas common-law judges might limit the persecutory zeal of the government and the complaisance of the local judiciary. I no longer believe that this is realistic. After years of mounting concern, the conviction of the fourteen democracy activists in May pushed me over the edge. I cannot bring myself to be part of a system in which respectable politicians may rot in jail for many years for using peaceful, and in my view lawful, constitutional means to advance the cause of democracy, something that the Basic Law itself acknowledges as its ultimate objective. I would not wish to be a judge in mainland China, and mainland China is the model towards which Hong Kong seems to be moving.

LAW IN OUR LIVES

VI

THE LEGITIMACY OF LAW*

I want to address a question that judges rarely ask them-selves. Yet it is arguably the most fundamental question that one can ask about the making of law. Putting it at its most general (and abstract), the question is this: what is it that makes a law legitimate? Is it the intrinsic morality of that law? Or is it the consent of the community that enacts it? In an ideal world, people would always consent to morally admirable laws, and their political institutions would always reject immoral ones. But the world is not ideal, because morality is only one element, and not necessarily the most important element in the way that people think about laws. They are motivated by a variable mixture of wisdom and folly, of prejudice and understanding, of idealism, pragma-tism and self-interest. To take just one example, although it is a topical and important one, some people may say that morality requires the admission into rich Western countries like ours of destitute refugees from war-torn countries of the world. Others would argue that there is no moral right to occupy someone else's space, no moral right, in other words, to migrate into the settled territory of another society. But what if people reject immigration on grounds that have nothing to do with morality, and everything to do with their

---

* *This lecture, originally delivered at the Aldeburgh Literary Festival in March 2020, reprises some of the themes examined in my BBC Reith Lectures of 2019.*

desire not to have to share their good fortune? They may wish to conserve their ethnic or cultural identity, their standard of living, their residential space, or their access to scarce resources such as transport, housing or education. Does consent trump morality, or is it the other way round? And if morality prevails, how do we resolve disagreements about what morality requires?

In a democracy there is a major fault line. Are there some laws that democratic legislatures should not be allowed to pass? Is it a proper function of judges to mould the law in accordance with some moral preference and, if so, whose moral preference? The growing importance of judicial lawmaking makes it important to answer these questions. Public law provides judges with many tools for giving effect to their own moral preferences and their own views about the public interest. A statute may be judged insufficiently clear to bear a meaning to which the judges object. Or people may be judged to have a 'legitimate expectation' which prevails over government policy. Or the concept of irrationality, a well-established ground of objection to the decisions of public authorities, may be stretched to encompass anything that the judge regards as unreasonable by their own lights. Policy decisions or public consultations may be found defective for not sufficiently addressing some objection entertained by the judge hearing the case. In areas such as immigration control, criminal sentencing and social security, the public does not share the liberal line that is fairly consistently taken by the judges.

In modern times, by far the most important tool available to judges for giving effect to their own policies has been the European Human Rights Convention. A democracy can legislate whatever rights it wants. The object of the Convention is to require signatory states to have certain rights that it may not want. It requires rights to be available irrespective of whether there is any democratic demand for them. It insists on some rights to which there may be strong democratic hostility. I have no problem about the rights spelled out in the Convention. But the Convention hands over two critically important powers to the courts and in particular to the European Court of Human Rights in Strasbourg. The first is a power to develop the rights in the Convention by a process of extrapolation and analogy, so as to encompass many things that are simply not there and have never been agreed by the subscribing states. The second is a power to decide when these rights should be overridden by some competing public interest, such as the suppression of crime or public health or the rights of others. These are both intensely political powers. Their transfer to the courts has of course been approved by Parliament in the Human Rights Act, but that is irrelevant to my point. If a democratic legislature authorises a new method of making legislative and political decisions, it is still relevant to ask whether that method is itself democratic. It seems to me to be beyond serious argument that the withdrawal of significant issues into a forum where the electorate has no say is not consistent with democracy. You can argue about whether that is a good or a bad thing, but you cannot rationally deny that it is happening. The way that laws are made for our society matters. It matters at least as much as the question of what laws are made.

I am going to start with a small dose of autobiography. I have spent most of my life as a practising lawyer. But I was not always a lawyer. I began my career as an academic historian. I read history at Oxford and taught the subject as a fellow of an Oxford college for much of my twenties. I left Oxford at the age of twenty-seven to retrain as a lawyer. But the habit of thinking historically about social problems persisted. One result is that I have always tended to look at law from the outside. Another is that I have not always accepted the political and moral pretensions of law as readily as some of my colleagues. Law is a priestly craft. It has its own language, its own conventions and its own values. It is a possessive profession, uniquely confident in the efficacy of legal solutions, intellectually self-assured and self-contained. In the Oxford history school, I was required to study the history of England as the organic development of a national community from the departure of the Romans to the twentieth century. I am eternally grateful to the late Victorian pedagogues who devised the syllabus. One of its advantages was that I came to realise how very small a contribution to the development of any society is ever made by a single generation, let alone any individual. Societies are not transformed, except by violence, and not always then. They evolve. The continuities are always more important than the changes. This has engendered in me a profound scepticism about the capacity of people to reshape the destinies of their world in accordance with their own preferences, moral or otherwise. In particular, although abstract thinking matters, it contributes less to the development of societies than instinct and experience.

In our lifetimes, law has become an increasingly idealistic discipline. It has been dominated by the concept of rights. Of course rights against other individuals have always been the stuff of law. We have contracts, torts, trusts, and so on, which fill the law books and the prospectuses of university law faculties. But the rights which have come to dominate the discourse of lawyers are rights in public law: human rights, political rights, social rights. These are rights nominally enforceable against the government, but in fact against the community at large. Let us call them public rights.

There is nothing wrong with public rights. There is nothing wrong with having more of them. The question with which I am concerned is how we should decide what public rights to have. The traditional answer to that question is that we should choose our public rights politically, through a representative legislature. The alternative, which is proposed by many lawyers and has become increasingly influential, is that while the legislature is certainly entitled to create public rights, there is a body of rights and laws that exists independently of political choice, and it falls to professional judges to identify and enforce them. At its most basic level, the controversy is between two models of the state, a legal model and a political one. The legal model, classically represented by the United States, calls for a constitution based on a framework of supreme rights, enforceable in the courts and practically beyond the reach of political interference. The judges decide what those rights are; the judges decide what they mean; the judges enforce them; and the judges have the ultimate authority to determine when the state may depart from them in some overriding public interest. The alternative is a political constitution, which treats all of these things as matters for decision by Parliament, or by ministers answerable to Parliament and ultimately to the electorate. The political model regards the community as absolutely entitled, through its collective decision-making machinery, to decide by what common rules it will be governed, and when it will depart from them according to its own conception of the collective interest.

The legal model is difficult to accommodate within the basic architecture of the British constitution. Britain is one of the few countries in the world whose constitution is not contained in a charter of supreme law. Its Parliament has unlimited legislative power. There is nothing that it cannot authorise, if necessary by a majority of one in each House. The limits on its action are political and practical, not constitutional. There is no foundational instrument by reference to which its legislation can be judged as deficient. Its proceedings and its legislation are alike immune from judicial review. The common law has recognised these principles, but it did not create them. They exist because, alone of the mature states of the world, there has been no break in Britain's constitutional history, no conquest since the eleventh century, no revolution since the middle of the seventeenth century, no moment of destruction and reconstruction. No other body has ever come into being to stand above Parliament since it took control of the prerogatives of the King in the eighteenth century.

Parliament's unlimited legislative jurisdiction means that one Parliament cannot bind itself or its successors. This is not a constitutional limit on its powers. It is simply a consequence of the absence of such a limit. Because Parliament is constitutionally supreme, it cannot be prevented from undoing the work of its predecessors. Thus, when the Fixed Term Parliaments Act 2011 provided that an early election could not be called without the approval of a two-thirds majority of the House of Commons, all that was required to circumvent it was a new Act providing for an early general election in 2019. The 2011 Act was repealed by ordinary legislation in 2020. It follows that in Britain there is no way of entrenching any rule of law, no way of placing it beyond the reach of political interference by a future parliamentary majority. The only way that this has ever been achieved is by conferring overriding legislative power on a body standing outside the constitutional framework of the United Kingdom. Even that is imperfect. The European Communities Act 1972 conferred overriding legislative and judicial power on the institutions of what is now the European Union. But what Parliament granted, Parliament could take away, as we have seen. The Human Rights Act 1998 in effect required the British courts to follow the decisions of the European Court of Human Rights in Strasbourg, but its decisions do not bind Parliament and it is only by political convention that Parliament will amend domestic law to bring it into line with Strasbourg jurisprudence. Any limits on Parliament's legislative powers are voluntary, and subsist only as long as Parliament decides.

Suppose that it were constitutionally possible to limit Parliament's legislative jurisdiction. Should we want to do it? The fundamental principle which underlay my Reith Lectures was that with limited exceptions the legal model of the constitution, with its recognised body of entrenched fundamental law, is inconsistent with the democratic state, or indeed with any form of social organisation ultimately based on consent. Constitutionally entrenched rights are creatures of their age, and may not reflect the values of another generation, or they may retain their value but need to be overridden in the interest of a wider range of countervailing public interests, something which calls for a political judgment. The main function of lawmakers is not to formulate moral ideals, and certainly not moral ideals for future generations. Their main purpose is to accommodate divergent interests and opinions among imperfect, disputatious and generally self-interested human beings, in order to enable them to live together in a political community without the systematic application of coercion.

To achieve that, law has to have legitimacy. Legitimacy is based on a collective loyalty to a method of making law. It is a shared sentiment that we owe it to each other to respect laws made by that method, even when we disagree with them. Legitimacy is the foundation of any civil society not based simply on force. There are distinguished philosophers who have argued that what makes a law legitimate is its intrinsic rationality or moral merit. According to this view, there is a body of public rights that can be discovered by pure reason, quite independently of any human institutions. The

American philosophers John Rawls and Ronald Dworkin were responsible for what are perhaps the most impressive essays of this kind. Rawls argued that legitimate laws were not the ones that societies actually chose, but the laws that they would notionally have chosen if people were ignorant of their own character and talents, so that they had no idea whether or not the laws would be in their interest. Dworkin argued that rights existed independently of human preferences, and could be said to exist even if no one believed in them or even knew about them. Common to both thinkers, and to all attempts to arrive at rights by a process of pure reason, is the view that collective consent is irrelevant. I have never found any of these theories persuasive. It is partly that they beg the question. They assume that the most legitimate law is the one that rationally proceeds from some moral premise, such as equality or fairness. They ignore the basic requirement of any law, which is that it should enable us to live together in society. Law does not exist in the abstract. It is a product of human social organisation. We cannot make a constitution for some imaginary world in which people are without prejudices or indifferent to their own interests. All that a political system can really aspire to do is to provide a method of decision-making that has the best chance of satisfying the needs of citizens as they actually are.

There are, I think, only two possible sources of legitimacy for law. One is ideology. The other is consent. In most places, and at most times, the legitimacy of law has depended on ideology. Divine endorsement, either of the law or of the kings who made it, is an ideology. It was the commonest source of legitimacy until modern times. But there have been other less benign sources of legitimacy. Communism, Fascism, Catholicism, Islamism, and a variety of nationalist ideologies have all at one time or another served to legitimise laws that were not based on consent. These were idealistic creeds that sought to impose on men and women some form of arbitrarily conceived moral perfection. All of them depended ultimately on the systematic application of coercion.

We are, or at least profess to be, a democracy. It is fundamental to the democratic constitution that it provides a consensual process of decision-making but does not prescribe what the outcome of that process should be. Politics is the only mechanism that we have for determining what the outcome should be by a process of collective consent. I do not idealise politics. I do not say that politics always does the job well. That would be absurd. I do say that it always does it better than judicial decision-making, because judicial decision-making is essentially non-consensual. The judiciary is not a representative body. It is not removable. And is not accountable to the electorate for what it does. Nor should it be.

If you are going to set up a body of principle which prevails over democratic choice, you have to ask yourself: what is it that makes those principles legitimate, if not democratic choice? The political world is full of people who believe that some rights are so obviously just that democratic choice should not be able to oust them. So be it, but what if some people disagree about what is just or obvious? Suppose, hypothetically, that I believe that there is or should be a legal right to medically assisted suicide. I say that this is essential to the dignity of human beings, and to their fundamental right to determine their own fate. Suppose, hypothetically, that you disagree. You say that the availability of suicide as an exit route would undermine the dignity and autonomy of the old and terminally ill, by subjecting them to insidious and unseen pressures to do away with themselves. If you are religious, you might add that your life does not belong only to yourself but also to God or those close to you. How are we to resolve this disagreement other than by a democratic process? Take another example. Surveillance operations and the keeping of records by the police or the security services have been held to be covered by the right of privacy protected by Article 8 of the Human Rights Convention. In practice, the argument is invariably about whether some methods of law enforcement are justified by the competing public interest in public safety. Successive decisions of the Strasbourg Court and the domestic courts have taken a very restrictive view of that exception. They have severely limited the right of the police and the security services to retain DNA records, to monitor internet or mobile phone contacts, to photograph people demonstrating in public streets, or to keep personal files on them. Some of these decisions have significantly inhibited the ability of the police to prevent or detect crime. This is a classic public policy dilemma. How much privacy are we prepared to sacrifice in the interest of detecting actual or potential crimes that undermine our security? There are single-issue pressure groups that come close to regarding privacy as an absolute value, interference with which can never be justified by considerations of public safety or national security. There are others who think that we should be prepared to submit to any intrusion that may make us safer. Most of us probably stand somewhere between these extremes. The point is that this cannot properly be regarded as a question of law. It is something on which we disagree among ourselves and we need a political process to resolve that difference. The result will not necessarily be the same in, say, Germany, with its difficult recent experience of the police state, as it is in Italy, which defeated the Red Brigades in the 1970s largely by highly intrusive methods of surveillance. These things are extraordinarily sensitive to public sentiment, to institutional standards, and to national culture and historic experience.

A believer in fundamental rights might say that democracy should be limited by certain values. But why is it legitimate that those values should be yours rather than mine? The only possible answer that either of us can give to that question is that our own view is legitimate because we think that it is obviously right. But that of course is the very point at issue. Ultimately, those who believe that there are values that should prevail over democratic choice are driven to say that some peoples' views should be imposed on everyone else. Yet if you dispense with consent, the question whose views ought to prevail remains unanswered. It becomes just a competition in the use of influence or force.

It is traditional, at this point of the argument, to ask what we would do if the majority were to vote a party into power on a programme of persecuting racial minorities, or enacting laws against religious apostasy, or instituting compulsory euthanasia, or whatever other barbarous programme might catch the public's fancy for the moment. I think we have to accept that our fellow citizens have the constitutional right in a democracy to do things that we abhor, and trust them not in practice to do so. Beyond a certain point, if they insist on doing them, society will break up or become a despotism. We have to trust in our powers of persuasion, even if experience shows that our fellow citizens are not always persuaded by propositions that we regard as self-evident. We have to accept these things because otherwise we cannot live together in a single political community with other people of diverse interests and opinions. Historical experience tends to suggest that these barbarities are not adopted by democracies. They are adopted by groups who need to suppress democratic institutions in order to give effect to their programme. Hitler came to power by a democratic process, but his wickedest acts were possible because he suppressed democratic processes in Germany. There is no historical inevitability about this. I decline to design a constitution for this country on the footing that my fellow citizens are monsters of prejudice and social destruction. Once one accepts that as the premise, then the whole point of living in society disappears.

These considerations apply generally to democracies, but they have a particular resonance in Britain, because of the way in which our institutions have developed. Britain is a parliamentary democracy in a more fundamental sense than is commonly realised. The whole structure of our institutions depends on the legislative and political sovereignty of Parliament. Those who would defend the imposition of judicial values on the making of law generally do so in one of two ways. Either they redefine democracy as a system of values that they associate with judicial lawmaking and of which they happen to approve; or else they criticise representative democracy itself on the grounds that it does not always achieve the results that they regard as desirable. All of us, however, have to face one basic reality. For Britain, Parliament is the only show in town. We are only a democracy because Parliament makes laws, and because ministers are answerable to Parliament for the formation and execution of policy. Parliament may not always be as effective or as popular as it should be. But the House of Commons is the only institutional means by which the electorate can influence policy. The appropriation by the courts of the right to decide what public morality requires, or where the public interest lies, cuts across lines of constitutional responsibility which are fundamental to our democracy.

I accept that there are limited categories of rights that are entitled to privileged status, and which democratic choice should not be allowed to displace. These are rights without which we cannot live in society at all. Thus there must be rights to be protected from arbitrary physical violence or arbitrary interference with life, liberty or property. Without these, social existence is nothing more than a competition in the exercise of raw power. There must also be rights of access to independent judges to vindicate these rights, administer the criminal law and enforce the limits of state power. In addition, I would accept that there are some rights which should have a privileged status because without them we cannot be a democracy: for example freedom of thought and speech, freedom of assembly, regular elections, and so on. I shall expand on these points in the next chapter. But apart from these rights, which are fundamental to the very existence of our society, I would distinguish between constitutional rules that determine how decisions are to be made, and constitutional rules that determine what the outcome of the decision-making process is to be. The first is a proper function of a democratic constitution and such rules ought to have a privileged status, by convention if not by law. The second is not a proper function of a democratic constitution. There should not be constitutional rules that require us to accept liberal values, although they happen to be my values. This is because it is inconsistent with the basic premise of liberal democracy for any values, including liberal ones, to be imposed by one group on another otherwise than by a process of collective consent. Liberals must apply their principles to their own beliefs and not just to those of other people.

The commonest and perhaps the most powerful argument against the view that I have been expressing is that law must be allowed to limit the impact of democratic legislation in order to protect minorities who get overlooked or ignored in the democratic process. In Britain, this is a solution without a problem. Except perhaps in Northern Ireland before 1972, Britain's parliamentary institutions have a good record for protecting the rights of minorities. The rights of employees, for example, originate in progressively expanding schemes of legislation starting in the 1830s, at a time when very few employees had votes and the main impetus behind protective legislation was moral sentiment. Judges have a more chequered record in this field. In both Britain and the United States employment protection was adopted by legislation at a time when the judiciary was profoundly suspicious of any interference with freedom of contract. Most questions involving the protection of minorities are questions of discrimination, whether by public authorities or private persons. We have perfectly adequate domestic laws to protect minorities against discrimination. Most human rights, however, have nothing to do with the protection of minorities. Freedom of thought and expression may sometimes protect minorities, and freedom of religion usually does. But if we take the most heavily litigated human rights, such as the right of privacy or the right to a court, these are concerned with the entrenchment of values that are wholly unrelated to the protection of minorities. They affect everyone. For advocates of judicial intervention, there is a broader concern which extends beyond minorities properly so-called. It is about what is sometimes called majoritarian tyranny: the abuse of parliamentary majorities to ride roughshod over the sensibilities of others. This is a problem that is inherent in democracy. Any controversial measure will have been opposed by a minority, which may regard it as immoral or even oppressive. But the political process is the only possible protection against that. Its essential function is not just to arrive at decisions but to accommodate dissent, something which generally involves compromise. Politics does not always do this well. But courts of law are indifferent to compromise and are impotent to deal with majoritarian tyranny, unless they assume general legislative powers in place of the elected legislature.

The other familiar argument in favour of entrenched rights is this: look, people say, at the wonderful decisions that the courts have made in this or that kind of case; look at the joy created by this or that right which would not exist but for the judges. This is rather like saying that despots may be bad but at least they make the trains run on time. It is essentially an argument that the end justifies the means, which is the argument of every despot that has ever lived. 'Look – they say – at the excellent things that we have done, which could never have been achieved by all those quarrelsome democratic legislators.' I would give three answers to this. Firstly, there is no right recognised by judges that could not equally have been conferred by ordinary domestic legislation, if there had been sufficient democratic appetite for it. Secondly, to say that judges make good law begs the question: what *is* good law? That is a question on which citizens may properly differ, in which case a political process is necessary to resolve that difference. Thirdly, to say that a legal rule originating in a judicial decision is a good rule begs the question as to whether it is so fundamental that we should have it irrespective of collective choice. We may like some of the laws that the courts have made, but we should not be indifferent to how they are made. If we dispense with collective consent in pursuit of a nobler morality, we will end up with institutions that dispense with consent in pursuit of other ends that we may regard as utterly ignoble.

VII

ENTRENCHING RIGHTS: THE RULE
OF LAW AND HUMAN RIGHTS*

The rule of law is one of the most familiar catchphrases in the legal vocabulary. It trips off the tongue without always provoking much reflection on its meaning. A concept that can be invoked with equal solemnity by President Biden and President Putin, by President Mugabe and Mrs Thatcher, by President Khatami of Iran and President von der Leyen of the European Union, must necessarily have a certain elasticity. All of these very different leaders have claimed to preside over states governed by the rule of law. The main question that divides them is the place of rights in their view of the world.

It has become traditional to refer to the rival approaches to the rule of law as the 'thin' and the 'thick' definition. The thin definition is essentially procedural. It would require only that the laws should be publicly accessible, should not be retrospective, and should apply generally, for example to the government as well as well as the citizen. The 'thick' definition would require the law to have a substantive content conferring a minimum of rights on individuals. These rights are generally identified with those proclaimed in classic

---

* *This piece originated as a lecture delivered to the Legal Research Foundation of New Zealand, in Auckland in October 2023.*

human rights instruments like the United Nations' Universal Declaration of Human Rights and the European Convention on Human Rights. Of course, this is an over-simplification. There are many positions between these extremes. But it will do for the moment.

Until recently, the thin definition held the field. The phrase 'the rule of law' was first coined by the Victorian scholar A. V. Dicey. Dicey's great work on the law of the constitution was published in 1885. In successive editions it remained the bible of British constitutional lawyers for many years. His definition of the rule of law was strictly procedural. It meant that no one could be penalised except in accordance with some established legal rule and that no one was above the law. But if Dicey invented the phrase to describe what we would now call the thin definition, the concept was much older. It dates back at least to Aristotle, who distinguished between the rule of laws and the rule of men. The rule of men depended on the changeable whims of the ruler. It was essentially discretionary and therefore arbitrary and unconfined. By comparison, the rule of laws provided a common template against which to measure the conduct of every man, including the ruler. It made law predictable.

The leading modern exponent of the thin definition was the late professor Joseph Raz. Professor Raz died in 2022 after a distinguished career culminating in his two decades as Professor of the Philosophy of Law at Oxford. He was a pupil of Herbert Hart and like him a legal positivist. Raz taught that the rule of law meant, first, that people should be ruled by law rather than governmental discretion, and, second, that the law should be such that people are able to be guided by it. In other words, it should be stable, publicly accessible, clear and not retrospective, and it should be applied by independent judges in accordance with fair procedures. That was all. In Raz's view, it had no substantive content. The rule of law was not necessarily the same thing as the rule of good law. It should not therefore be confused with democracy, justice, equality or human rights. These things might be highly desirable but they were not implicit in the idea of the rule of law. Raz took his view to its logical conclusion. He once observed that a state that instituted slavery by law would be a wicked state but it would not infringe the rule of law.

The thick definition became increasingly influential after the Second World War as a result of attempts to codify fundamental human rights. This was largely a reaction to the atrocities of the totalitarian states of the interwar and wartime periods. One of the earliest formulations, and certainly one of the most expansive, is to be found in the 1959 statement of the International Congress of Jurists meeting in Delhi. This declared that the function of the legislator in a society governed by the rule of law was 'to create and maintain the conditions which will uphold the dignity of man as an individual'. This dignity, they continued, 'requires not only a recognition of his civil and political rights but also the establishment of the social, economic, educational and cultural conditions which are essential to the full development of his personality.'

The thick definition of the rule of law is probably the prevailing one today. It is endorsed by most common-law judges who have pronounced on the subject. Lord Bingham, a former senior law lord, was the author of one of the most ambitious modern attempts at a comprehensive definition. In his book *The Rule of Law*, published in 2010, he argued that the rule of law embraced the entire code of rights contained in the European Convention on Human Rights, essentially on the grounds that they were to be regarded as 'the basic entitlements of a human being'. In New Zealand, substantially the same view was expressed in a notable lecture delivered two years ago by Justice Susan Glazebrook. She considered that the rule of law was a guiding principle, so long as it included (among other things) human rights and redress for historical disadvantage. The rule of law, she suggested, was 'a catch cry for a better and more just world'. These statements, like the Delhi Declaration of 1959, suggest that the rule of law requires one to treat the law not just as a framework for decision-making but as an active agent of social improvement.

The problem with this debate is that we are in danger of becoming the prisoners of artificial categories and of asking the wrong questions. When an idea like the rule of law acquires supreme intellectual prestige and universal support, there is a natural tendency to expand its definition so as to embrace all sorts of other things which a legal philosopher may like to see but which are more controversial. This is what has happened to the concept of the rule of law. We are inclined to give it whatever meaning accords with the kind of laws we would like to have. The real question is what rights are truly fundamental to the subsistence of civil society so that they should not depend on political choice. It does not matter what label we give them.

Let us start from first principles. The rationale of international human rights law is that there are some rights which are inherent in our humanity. They should not therefore depend on the collective choices of the societies to which we happen to belong. Instruments such as the Universal Declaration are content to assert this. The most interesting attempt to justify it has come from the Anglo-American legal philosopher Ronald Dworkin. Dworkin was one of a number of philosophers of the post-war period who tried to find an objective test for determining what moral claims human beings have against society. He and John Rawls were perhaps the best known of them. Dworkin argued that there were binding principles of public morality that were objectively true and should be enforced by judges, independently of the choices or opinions of the societies which they served. These principles of public morality, he said, would be just as true even if nobody believed them or even knew about them. It might be difficult to know what they were. But, like the truth about the origin of the universe or the composition of the stars, the truth about moral principles exists somewhere out there. Because some rights exist independently of human institutions and human choices, they are necessarily fundamental.

As a rhetorical tour de force, Dworkin's books and lectures are in a class of their own. But I do not accept his central thesis. Moral principles do not exist in a vacuum any more than rights do. They are products of the human mind. They are inherently sensitive to experience and to the premise, often instinctive, from which one starts. In what sense can such principles be said to exist independently of the opinions of men and women? How are we to determine objective truth in an area so redolent of subjective judgment, imperfect observation and flawed reasoning? But the main problem about Dworkin's ideas is a different one. They do not cater for the possibility of disagreement. There are profound differences of opinion among serious analytical thinkers as well as ordinary citizens about what the true moral principles are and in what circumstances if any we are morally entitled to qualify them. Dworkin reasons his way towards a number of moral rules. But if we disagree with his premises, his reasons or his conclusions, how are we to resolve the issue if not by making a collective choice, in other words through some kind of political process?

All laws require some source of legitimacy. We have to have a reason for complying with laws that we disagree with, other than mere state coercion. In a democracy, the legitimacy of the laws depends on their having been enacted or approved (expressly or tacitly) by some accepted legislative process, i.e. by collective choice. If you want to create a body of law that is independent of collective choice, you have to identify some other source of legitimacy for these rights apart from the institutional arrangements by which we are governed. There has to be some transcendent authority independent of our political institutions. For most of human history, rights were regarded as part of the moral law, ordained by God. The legitimacy of laws depended on the divine authority that monarchs claimed for themselves and their decrees. In our own day, and for at least a century past, the alternative to collective consent as a source of legitimacy has been ideology, in practice the ideology of some ruling group. These are all highly authoritarian systems.

I would identify two categories of rights which are truly fundamental and should not therefore depend on political choice.

First of all, there are rights without which life would be nothing more than a crude contest in the deployment of force: freedom from coercion except by established legal authority, freedom from arbitrary detention, physical violence, injury or death, recourse to impartial and independent courts. These are rights which are clearly implicit in the rule of law. They are quite close to Professor Raz's thin definition. But I think that a better way of explaining them is that without them social existence is not possible. If life is just a contest in the deployment of force, there is no society. The basic bonds of human solidarity that make a society cannot exist in those conditions.

There is a second category of rights which I would also regard as fundamental. It comprises rights without which our society cannot function as a democracy. I do not believe that democracy is a necessary part of the rule of law. Britain enjoyed the rule of law long before it was a democracy. The same is true of most Western countries, which had orderly systems of law before they ever had universal suffrage. But I add this second category of rights for a different reason. The distinction between rights which are fundamental and those which are merely optional is only relevant in a democracy. The reason why we make this distinction is that we believe that some rights should be protected against encroachments by politicians and other critics who may be able to garner majority support. The *Federalist Papers*, which Alexander Hamilton, James Madison and John Jay wrote to promote the ratification of the 1787 Constitution of the United States, remain to this day among the most influential analyses of this dilemma. They are largely concerned with the need to place constitutional limits on the measures that an electoral majority might otherwise be able to force through. Hamilton and his colleagues were troubled mainly by the debt forgiveness statutes that a number of states had passed in the interest of debtors, who constituted a larger part of the electorate than creditors. In the past century we have had plenty of reminders of much more extreme measures which democratic majorities can authorise. Hitler in Germany and Pétain in France were both granted irrevocable and unlimited powers by democratic legislatures. Even in less extreme circumstances, democratic legislatures have authorised a variety of arbitrary or oppressive laws. So I would add to the category of fundamental rights freedom of thought and expression, assembly and association in their broadest sense, and the right to participate on equal terms with everyone else in fair and regular elections. It also follows that people must have sufficient liberty to make use of these rights. These rights are not part of the rule of law, but they are fundamental for the same reason as the rule of law is fundamental. They are the necessary foundation of every human society founded on democratic decision-making.

Everything else, apart from these two categories, is open

to legitimate debate and is therefore properly the subject of democratic choice through a political process. This is of course a more limited view of fundamental rights than many people would wish. It leaves out many things which they would regard as important: privacy, race relations, same-sex partnerships, penal policy, immigration, education and social benefits, to name only those that have proved most controversial. The Universal Declaration of Human Rights includes in its catalogue of human rights a right to social security, fair remuneration for work done, an adequate standard of living, and free education. These are all admirable aspirations. But in a democracy they must depend on political choice. Otherwise, almost all social policy would be determined by the courts rather than the political forum of the nation.

There are good reasons why a democracy should take a narrower view of fundamental rights than the Universal Declaration, and good reasons why it should be cautious about entrenching any rights outside the two categories which I have identified. International human rights are generally born of a suspicion of democratic decision-making. Those who would like to see rights to a better world given the status of fundamental law, generally do so because they fear that democratic electorates will never be morally pure enough to adopt them voluntarily. Their fears are in a sense justified. The decisions of voters are *not* morally pure. They are based at least in part on self-interest. But that cannot be a good enough reason to constrain their choices by law. The interests and opinions of citizens conflict. We cannot all have our own way. All that we can reasonably expect is that collective decisions will be made in accordance with a procedure that treats our various interests and opinions with equal consideration and respect. That is achieved by giving all of us an equal share in decision-making even if, as individual voters, our personal influence on the outcome is minimal. Outside the two categories, rights are necessarily open to dispute and are often hotly disputed in practice. Disputable rights cannot be imposed in a system based on consent. The dispute has to be resolved through our mechanisms for collective consent.

In sum, I suggest that the essence of democracy is not moral rectitude but participation. We need a method of decision-making that has the best chance of accommodating disagreements between citizens as they actually are. This calls for a political process in which every citizen can engage, and whose results, however imperfect, are likely to be acceptable to the widest possible range of interests and opinions. This is surely a much more important priority for a political community than finding some objectively just answer to its moral dilemmas. Legally entrenched rights marginalise the political process. They involve the creation of a class of rights whose existence and extent are not to be determined by political choice. That has serious implications, of which our societies are not sufficiently conscious. Of course we need a minimum of rights in order to function as a democracy. But if we place too many rights beyond the reach of democratic choice, we may cease to be a democracy just as surely as if we had no rights at all.

The debate in the United States about abortion conveniently illustrates these themes. I am in favour of a regulated right of abortion. But that is a moral and political choice that others would disagree with. I question whether abortion can properly be treated as a fundamental right, displacing political choice. Abortion was once just as controversial in Britain as it still is in the United States. After extensive parliamentary debate, it was introduced in 1967 by ordinary legislation, within carefully defined limits and subject to a framework of clinical regulation. The same pattern was followed in the rest of Europe, where all but one state have now legislated for a regulated right of abortion. One reason why abortion remains so controversial in the United States is that it was introduced by the US Supreme Court in *Roe v Wade* 410 US 113 (1973), as a judicial interpretation of the constitution, i.e., by a method that rendered irrelevant the wider political debate among Americans. This means that a framework of clinical regulation is hard to achieve, since it would operate to limit a constitutional right. It also means that the right to abortion is the supreme law of the land, unless and until the Constitution is amended or the Supreme Court changes its mind. Constitutional amendment is practically impossible in the US system. A change of mind on the part of the Supreme Court is rare. It recently happened in *Dobbs v Jackson Womens' Health Organisation* 597 US 215 (2022), when the US Supreme Court overruled its own decision in *Roe v Wade*. There are serious doubts about the propriety of *Dobbs*. In a precedent-based system it is usually wrong to overrule a decision of the highest court that had stood for half a century in the absence of some material change in the intervening period. The only change in this instance was that a politically motivated bench did not like the earlier decision. But the principle in *Dobbs*, that decriminalising abortion was a matter for democratic legislatures, cannot be faulted.

The justification commonly put forward for treating such matters as constitutional issues for the courts is that it protects minorities against majoritarian tyranny better than the legislative process. I question whether there is any factual basis for this assumption in stable democracies. What constitutes majoritarian tyranny very much depends on how you define your minority and what you regard as tyranny. Except perhaps in classic discrimination cases, where the animating principle is to treat like cases alike, there are no legal standards by which these questions can be answered. The only available standards are political. Experience suggests that judges charged with making essentially political decisions are no more likely than professional politicians to make enlightened ones. There is also, perhaps, a wider issue, namely, whether it is wise to make law in a way that marginalises the choices of the electorate. In the United States it has done great damage, polarising opinion and turning presidential elections into contests for the right to appoint suitably biased Supreme Court justices.

In our societies, we have too much confidence in judge-made law as an agent of social change. We need to value and defend truly fundamental rights, but we also need to understand the moral and practical limits of what law can achieve. In the end, law simply has no solution to the problem of majoritarian tyranny, even in a system of perfectly entrenched constitutional rights like that of the United States. Law can insist that public authorities have some legal basis for everything that they do. It can supply the basic level of security on which civilised life depends. It can protect minorities identified by some personal characteristic, such as gender, race or sexual orientation, from discrimination on those grounds. But law cannot parry the broader threat that legislative majorities may act oppressively, unless judges assume general legislative powers for themselves. The only effective constraints on the abuse of democratic power are political. Politics may be a dirty word, but the alternative to politics is bleak: an authoritarian model of the state, leading to a dysfunctional community and exposed to mounting internal and external violence. In the United States this is a potential catastrophe in the making. But there is nothing that law can do about it. As Montesquieu pointed out three centuries ago, the spirit of the laws matters a lot more than anything that law can ever guarantee.

VIII

THE PRESIDENT'S CRIMES*

Aristotle's distinction between the rule of laws and the rule of men has left a long legacy. Laws, said the great sage, are considered, rational rules that apply generally. The rule of a man, by comparison, is an invitation to government by discretion and, ultimately, to tyranny. 'He who would have the rule of a man adds an element of the beast,' he wrote, 'for desire is a wild beast, and passion perverts the minds of rulers, even when they are the best of men. The law is reason unaffected by desire.'

There is no country in which this distinction is more important than the United States in the age of Donald Trump. Article II of the Constitution concentrates all civil and military power in the hands of the president. He appoints all federal officers, subject in some cases to the approval of the Senate. Once appointed, these officers are the president's agents, holding office at his pleasure and acting on his instructions. The president derives his powers directly from the Constitution and is not answerable to Congress except by way of impeachment. All this is consistent with responsible government but only because the president is subject to law. The great case of *Marbury v Madison* (1803) is generally regarded as the foundation of American public

* *This is a lightly edited version of an article that originally appeared in the October 2024 edition of* Prospect.

law. Delivering the judgment of the Supreme Court, Chief Justice Marshall observed that

> the government of the United States has been emphatically termed a government of laws, and not of men. It will certainly cease to deserve this high appellation if the laws furnish no remedy for the violation of a vested legal right.

One can only speculate on what Marshall would have thought about the judgment of his successors in *Trump v United States*, which was handed down on 1 July 2024. The Court has held that Trump is immune from prosecution for criminal acts committed in the course of his official functions as President, even after he has left office. It has returned the case to the District Court to decide whether the acts alleged against Trump were or were not done in the course of his official functions. But they have added some highly expansive criteria that bring many criminal acts within the scope of his official functions. The Court was at pains to say that the issue should be addressed as a matter of principle and not just in the light of the circumstances of the case. But it is fair to say that the circumstances of the case were a stiff test of their decision.

A federal grand jury had indicted Trump for conspiring to overturn the result of the 2020 presidential election. The indictment accused him of trying to do this by using allegations of election fraud that he knew to be groundless in order to get state officials to change Biden votes into Trump votes; by getting the Department of Justice to start sham criminal investigations into non-existent election frauds; by having bogus electoral college members put forward for certification by his Vice President; by pressuring his Vice President to reject the results from swing states that went for Biden;

and finally by directing a violent mob of his supporters to the Capitol to bring pressure to bear on the Vice President. The grand jury had concluded that on the face of it these allegations were supported by the evidence. For the purposes of the appeal, it had to be assumed that they were correct, or at least that they might be. Most of them were matters of public record. The question was whether, even so, the prosecution should be barred.

The suggestion that Trump was immune from prosecution even if the allegations were true had been rejected with some indignation by the District Court and the Court of Appeals. If an ex-president is immune from criminal liability for trying to overthrow the Constitution and install an unelected intruder in the White House, one is bound to wonder what is left of the Constitution.

Before looking at how the Supreme Court arrived at this result, it helps to see how the law was generally understood before the judgment was handed down.

The first point to be made is that there is nothing about presidential immunity in the Constitution. The Framers knew how to include it, for they conferred some immunities on congressmen. The omission of a comparable immunity for presidents is not of course conclusive, but what we know about the Framers' intentions suggests that it was deliberate. They were English gentlemen who were perfectly familiar with the workings of the British constitution. They were well aware of the English legal maxim 'The King can do no wrong', and determined to have none of it. Blackstone's *Commentaries on the Laws of England*, then the most influential treatise on the common law on both sides of the Atlantic, had explained what this maxim meant. It meant that the King was sovereign and, by definition, no institution can stand above a sovereign. He could not therefore be sued or prosecuted in his own courts (although there were other ways in which civil relief could be obtained). It also meant that by a legal fiction the King was incapable of acting unlawfully, because any unlawful act was to be imputed to his advisers, generally ministers answerable to Parliament.

The Framers of the Constitution chose a form of government to which none of these notions could apply. The United States was to be a republic belonging to the sovereign people. The President was not a sovereign but an agent of the state. The courts were not his courts, but a co-equal branch of the state. The imputation of wrongs to advisers and ministers, which was and is the cornerstone of English doctrine, made no sense in a constitution that had no equivalent of the English principle of ministerial responsibility. The United States has an executive President whose ministers and advisers are answerable to him and not to Congress. The danger of irresponsible government was allayed by the Constitution itself, which provided that it was to be 'the supreme law of the land'. In 1879 the Supreme Court reviewed these points in *Langford v United States* and concluded that the maxim that the King can do no wrong had no place in the American system of government.

There was (and still is) a well-established rule, dating back to *Marbury v Madison* itself, that the courts will not question acts of the executive that lie within the discretion conferred on the President by the Constitution or by statute. This is sometimes described as an immunity. In reality, however, it only means that acts of the President in the exercise of a discretion conferred on him by law are lawful. They cannot therefore give rise to liability, civil or criminal.

There is also a principle dating back to the 1890s that federal employees performing executive functions are immune from *civil* liability for damages arising from the performance of their duties. In *Nixon v Fitzgerald* (1982), the Supreme Court had applied this principle to any act of the President within the 'outer perimeter' of his official functions. So Arthur Fitzgerald, who had been dismissed from the Air Force by President Nixon in retaliation for unwelcome evidence that he had given to a congressional subcommittee, was denied a remedy. The Court's reasoning was based partly on the extreme breadth of the President's discretions in hiring and firing federal employees, partly on the public interest against distracting the President from constitutional duties, and partly on the Court's concern that unless he is immune he may perform his duties too cautiously for fear of provoking lawsuits. The principle has its limits, however. In two later cases, *Clinton v Jones* (1997) and *Trump v Vance* (2020), the Supreme Court explained that the mere fact that litigation was liable to distract the President from his official functions was not enough. The real objection to civil litigation against the President was said to be that the distraction might lead to overcautious decision-making. President Clinton no doubt found it most distracting to have to answer Paula Jones's claim for damages for sexual harassment, but that was irrelevant. He was not immune because, the alleged harassment having occurred long before he was elected, there was no question of overcautious decision-making.

Finally, there has for half a century been a convention that the President may not be criminally prosecuted during his term of office. The authority for it is rather thin. It consists of two opinions from the Office of Legal Counsel, part of the Department of Justice. The first was issued in 1973 when Nixon was being accused of obstructing the investigation of the Watergate break-in. The second was issued in 2000 when it was being alleged that Clinton had been party to a fraudulent property scheme when he was attorney general of Arkansas in 1978. Both opinions argued that the prosecution or conviction of a sitting president was unconstitutional because it would distract him from his duties, especially if he was jailed. There is no judicial or other legal authority that says this, but the opinions matter because they are treated as binding within the Department of Justice. This means that they govern prosecution policy. Rightly or wrongly, the Department does not prosecute sitting presidents.

One thing at least was clear. The Constitution itself provides that the President may be impeached and convicted in Congress for 'treason, bribery or other high crimes and misdemeanors'. Thus the President was plainly capable of criminal liability, and it had never been suggested that impeachment was the exclusive mode of enforcing that liability. Nor had anyone ever thought that presidents were immune from criminal liability after they had left office. Indeed, at Trump's second impeachment trial his own lawyers accepted this. They argued that by throwing out the charges the Senate would not be putting him above the law, because an ex-president 'is like any other citizen and can be tried in a court of law'.

This then was the background when the Supreme Court came to decide *Trump v United States*. The Court was divided. In a pattern that has unfortunately become routine, the majority comprised the six justices appointed by Republican presidents (subject to one reservation by Justice Barrett), while the three justices appointed by Democrat presidents all dissented. The majority judgment was delivered by Chief Justice Roberts. His reasoning was that the Constitution confers enormous powers on the President so that he will be in a position to take bold and decisive action in the interests of the nation. Therefore the *Fitzgerald* principle governing civil litigation against a current or former president should apply equally to criminal prosecutions. The threat of criminal prosecution, he held, was at least as likely to give rise to distraction and overcautious decision-making as the threat of civil litigation. The role of the courts must therefore be limited to deciding whether the relevant act was done in the performance of the President's official functions. If it was, then he was immune and that was an end of it.

For the lower courts, the answer had been perfectly straightforward. The President has no constitutional or statutory authority to commit crimes. So criminal acts are by definition not part of his official functions. In the Supreme Court, the majority thought that that was too simple. Courts, they said, cannot treat an act of the President as unofficial merely because some prosecutor has alleged that it violates the criminal law. But equally, courts cannot examine whether it actually did violate the criminal law. That might, for example, depend on the President's motive for doing the act or whether they knew the facts that made it illegal. The courts, said the majority, could not be allowed to investigate that, for doing so would give rise to the very risk of distraction and overcautious decision-making that the immunity was designed to avoid. All that they can decide is whether the relevant act falls within a class of acts that presidents do in their capacity as presidents. Thus the courts cannot be allowed to consider, for example, whether the President did the act because he had taken a bribe, because taking a bribe is by definition something that is done in the course of an official function.

The majority distinguished between those acts of the President that fell within his 'core' functions, and other acts that fell within their 'outer perimeter'. 'Core' functions were those, such as hiring and firing federal employees or issuing pardons, where the law confers an unrestricted discretion on the President to do a class of acts that only he can do. In these cases, the inquiry stops there. The President is absolutely immune. Cases falling within the 'outer perimeter' of the President's functions are those where the position is less clear. It may be difficult to know in what capacity the

President was acting, or which if any of his many powers he was exercising. In these cases, the majority held that the President was 'presumptively immune'. This meant that he was immune unless the prosecution could positively demonstrate that the relevant act did not belong to a class of acts that presidents can do, or perhaps that there was no danger of a distracting 'intrusion' on his attention. In plain language what this means is that because of the awesome powers and responsibilities of the President he must be allowed to do what he wants, without being unduly 'distracted' by the thought that it may be a criminal offence.

The majority did not say and cannot possibly have thought that it was part of the official functions of the President of the United States to try to overturn a regular election result and occupy the White House through what would have amounted to a coup. But instead of looking at the nature and object of the conspiracy alleged against Trump, their approach was to look separately at each of the things that he is alleged to have done to further it.

Thus the indictment alleged that Trump tried to get the Department of Justice to launch criminal investigations into non-existent election frauds. Discussing possible prosecutions with the department, said the majority, is the kind of thing that presidents do as part of their 'core' constitutional duty to 'take care that the laws be faithfully executed'. So those discussions are absolutely immune. The prosecution cannot be allowed to prove that in this particular case the discussions were actually about defeating the laws by mounting sham investigations. So by a perverse irony, the fact that the President has a duty to see to the observance of the law becomes a reason why he cannot be prosecuted for breaking it himself.

Then Trump is said to have tried to get swing states to falsify their election returns to the Senate, and to induce the

Vice President to reject the election results of some states that voted for Biden. These were not 'core' functions of the President. The preparation of election returns to the Senate was a function of the states, and certifying them was a function of the Vice President in his capacity as President of the Senate. So if the President interferes with them, he is only presumptively immune. Nonetheless, said the majority, discussing such matters with the state authorities and the Vice President might well be a presidential function. Never mind that these particular discussions were about falsifying the result of the elections. The courts cannot be allowed to look into questions like that.

The majority's most remarkable observations concern Trump's notorious tweets and public speech on 6 January 2021, in which he urged his supporters to head for the Capitol to pressurise the Vice President. The President, they declared, 'possesses extraordinary power to speak to his fellow citizens'. So if the Court finds that Trump was tweeting and speaking as President and not, say, as a party leader or candidate, then what he said was by its very nature immune. Never mind if the 'fellow citizens' whom he was addressing were an ugly mob whom he was inviting to invade the Capitol and threaten legislators with violence. The courts cannot be allowed to look into that either.

There are a number of problems here, apart from the absurdity of the result.

One is that the distinction between the kind of power that the President was exercising and the way that he was exercising it is incoherent. Often, the only way that you can decide whether an act of the President was done in the course of his official functions is to enquire why and how he did it. But that is the one thing that the judgment stops the courts from doing.

However, the fundamental difficulty with the reasoning

is that there is no analogy between the risk of civil litigation and the risk of criminal prosecution. Civil litigation is
designed to vindicate a private right of the plaintiff. Criminal prosecutions are an entirely different matter. They are
brought by the state to vindicate a public right, namely the
right to have the Constitution respected and the criminal law
observed. The law does sometimes override private rights in
the public interest. But the enforcement of the criminal law
against anyone, however mighty, and the protection of the
Constitution against a coup are public interests of an altogether higher order. Overriding them raises issues that go
to the root of the Constitution. The scale of the risk is also
very different. The United States is a litigious society. Anyone
with a grudge can get a lawyer on a contingency fee to bring
a civil complaint based on their own perhaps fanciful version
of the facts. This is not true of criminal prosecutions. Pros-
ecutors have important ethical obligations. They are subject
to administrative and professional disciplinary codes. They
must have reasonable and probable cause to believe that a
person has committed a crime before proceeding. Felonies
are the most serious category of crimes, and in the federal
system and most states a prosecutor must persuade a grand
jury that there is sufficient evidence on each count to justify
a prosecution. In the entire history of the United States, no
serving or former president has ever been indicted for criminal conduct in office until now, although Nixon probably
could have been if his successor had not pardoned him.

One might think that if there is reasonable and probable cause to believe that a president has committed crimes,
some investigation would be in order, however distracting,
so that the judicial branch of the state can perform its own
overriding duty to apply the law. However, the nub of the
majority's reasoning is not the issue of distraction. It is their
apparent concern that without immunity presidents may

be overcautious in their decisions. What is the basis for this concern? The short answer is that there is none. No empirical evidence or historical experience is cited in the majority judgment, and the suggestion is both factually implausible and conceptually bizarre. It is factually implausible because the risk of criminal prosecution does not seem to have led to overcautious decision-making by Trump himself or by any of his forty-four predecessors, even though it had always previously been assumed that presidents were exposed to prosecution for their crimes like anyone else. It is conceptually bizarre because when the judges talk of overcautious decision-making, they must mean an approach to decision-making that would be unduly influenced by the need to take extra care to avoid prosecution. But there is a much simpler way to avoid prosecution – namely to refrain from committing crimes. Unlike most civil liabilities, criminal liability almost always requires a guilty mind. There has to be proof of knowledge and intent. Presidents do not commit felonies by accident or without realising what they are doing. As for the risk of baseless accusations of criminality, if that really is a problem then no amount of caution in decision-making can avoid it.

The majority judges objected with some asperity to the suggestion by the dissenters that their judgment put the President above the law. But what other construction can be put upon their words? If there is no remedy against the President, then there is no law binding on him. The danger that presidents will change their approach to decision-making in order to avoid criminal liability seems remote. The danger that some presidents, freed from the prospect of criminal liability, will more readily turn to crime is surely much greater.

The Supreme Court has always been a very political court and usually a very conservative one. In *Dredd Scott v Sandford* (1857) the Court notoriously held that African Americans could not be citizens, contributing to the tensions that ultimately provoked the Civil War. After the Civil War, it conducted a rearguard action against the constitutional amendments and congressional acts that sought to outlaw discrimination against African Americans. During the so-called Lochner era between 1897 and 1937, it repeatedly struck down employment protection laws in the name of freedom of contract. It obstructed Roosevelt's New Deal for most of the 1930s. The Court's approach changed after the Second World War. The turning point was the appointment of Earl Warren as Chief Justice in 1953. A new generation of justices stood for a liberal agenda on racial segregation, civil rights and moral issues such as abortion. Some of their decisions were politically controversial. In particular, the decision of the Court in *Roe v Wade* (1973), recognising a constitutional right to abortion, polarised American opinion. It led directly to the adoption as part of the Republican Party's platform of a policy of packing the Court with justices who would reverse the liberal tide. As a result, presidential elections became a contest for the right to appoint sufficiently partisan justices to the Supreme Court. The Court became political in a new and more dangerous sense.

Before the 1990s, presidents had not always appointed justices who agreed with their own political outlook. Democrats sometimes appointed conservatives, and Republicans sometimes appointed liberals. Attempts to pack the Court usually failed because even politically sympathetic justices could be resolutely independent-minded after their appointment. Eisenhower appointed Earl Warren, a former Republican governor of California, in order to consolidate a conservative majority on the Court and was grievously disappointed by the result. 'I made two mistakes,' he famously declared some years later, 'and both of them are sitting on the Supreme Court.' (The other was Justice William Brennan).

Recent Republican presidents have learned from

Eisenhower's mistakes. The Federalist Society, a conservative legal pressure group founded in 1982, grooms convinced conservative lawyers from a young age for jobs in the federal judiciary. All six of the current conservative majority on the Supreme Court were either members of or closely associated with the Society. So were forty-three out of fifty-one of Trump's nominees to federal circuit courts of appeal. None of them has done a Warren. And since they are appointed for life, they will be around to preserve their appointer's legacy long after that person has left office. The position is aggravated by partisanship on the Senate Judiciary Committee, which must confirm appointments. Republican majorities on the committee delayed the confirmation hearings for Merrick Garland, Obama's last Supreme Court nomination, until Obama's term ended so that his Republican successor could fill the vacancy instead. They then accelerated the hearing of Amy Coney Barrett, Trump's last appointment, so as to get it confirmed before he left office.

Judges in whatever jurisdiction do not usually reason their way to a conclusion from first principles. They adopt a procedure somewhat like scientific research. They start with a hypothetical solution that reflects their instinctive view about what they would expect the law to be. They test it against the underlying legal principles and against the facts. If their instinctive answer does not stack up when subjected to these tests, they change their minds and try another one. The process is highly sensitive to the judge's instinctive starting point and to his or her willingness to ignore the difficulties. Constitutional judges who start from a pronounced political position need far greater intellectual self-discipline than others if they are to avoid discrediting their office. The conservative majority on the Court does not always side with Trump. In *Trump v Vance* (2020), a rare bipartisan decision, they rejected Trump's argument that as President he was immune from having to produce documents about his tax affairs in response to a New York subpoena. All of Trump's appointees signed up to that. But the conservative majority has consistently given the force of law to legally controversial Republican positions on, for example, abortion, gun control, election expenses, discriminatory voting rules, gerrymandering, and the powers of statutory executive agencies such as the Environmental Protection Agency. As a result, the Court's legitimacy has been gravely undermined and its public approval rating has collapsed from over 80 per cent in the 1990s to less than 50 per cent now.

This is a more serious problem in the United States than it would be in any other country. Congress is polarised, dysfunctional and gridlocked. Filibusters make it difficult to get controversial legislation through. This leaves the Supreme Court as the only institution that can change the law on contentious issues. When the Supreme Court changes the law on constitutional grounds there is no democratic way to undo it. The Constitution is practically incapable of amendment without bipartisan support. It needs a two-thirds vote in each house of Congress and ratification by three-quarters of the states. The Court's decrees therefore determine what the Constitution means until the crack of doom. This is a problem almost unique among the world's constitutions.

The decision in *Trump v United States* is merely the most recent and extreme symptom of a profound constitutional disorder in the affairs of the United States. The Constitution is the oldest written constitution in the world, but it is a fair-weather instrument. The United States is fortunate in having enjoyed a great deal of fair weather in the course of its history. But that may now be coming to an end. The elaborate system of checks and balances can work only if there is common ground across the political spectrum that the end does not always justify the means. There has to be a culture in which politicians regard it as more important to make the Constitution work in the interest of all parties than for any one party to get its way by hook or by crook. The fault is not all on one side of the political divide. But the Republican Party's sense of political entitlement, its ruthless constitutional obstructiveness and its irrational rage against Democrat presidents Clinton and Obama have junked the political culture that made the Constitution workable. President Biden's proposal that the President should appoint one justice every two years to sit for a limited term of eighteen years is a sensible start, but the Democrats would need an electoral landslide for it to have any chance of getting through Congress. Biden's proposal to amend the Constitution to make presidents answerable for their crimes is at once essential and impossible. The United States has never stood in greater need of impartial constitutional arbiters in its highest court, and has never been further from getting them.

THE INTERNATIONAL
DIMENSION OF LAW

IX

INTERNATIONAL TRIBUNALS:
FOR AND AGAINST*

The last half-century has witnessed an important new development in the constitutional life of the United Kingdom and many other Western countries: the growing importance of international tribunals as a source of domestic law.

International tribunals originated as a means of resolving disputes between states. Sovereign states are entities recognising no superior authority. Voluntary submission to some adjudicatory body is therefore the only alternative to interstate violence. This has been a feature of international relations since the world of the Greek city-states, and probably well before that. Until the end of the nineteenth century, the tribunals which adjudicated on interstate disputes were almost invariably ad hoc arbitrations with no continuing existence beyond the particular disputes referred to them. The most celebrated and influential example was the submission of the United Kingdom and the United States to an international arbitration to resolve the *Alabama* claims. The CSS *Alabama* was a commerce raider built at Birkenhead for the Confederacy during the American Civil War. The United States claimed damages on the basis that allowing it

---

* This is an expanded and updated version of a lecture given at an
international symposium organised by members of the Oxford Law Faculty in Budapest, in June 2023.

to leave England was a belligerent act inconsistent with the United Kingdom's neutrality. The tribunal, which included Sir Alexander Cockburn, Chief Justice of Queen's Bench, sat in Geneva. It ultimately decided in favour of the United States and awarded damages of $15.5 million, a very considerable sum at the time. At the same time the United States allowed nearly $2 million against this sum as damages due to the United Kingdom for its own illegal blockade practices. The balance was paid by Britain in 1872. Britain could have ignored the *Alabama* claims. There was very little that the United States could have done about it, short of going to war. Its submission to arbitration reflected a belief that a rule-based international order had long-term advantages for both states which transcended the immediate issues.

A major landmark in the adoption of a wider rule-based international order was the creation by the Hague Conference of 1899 of the Permanent Court of Arbitration. The modern successor of this body is the International Court of Justice, permanently housed in the Peace Palace at The Hague, with its own statutes, procedures and staff, including fifteen judges elected by the General Assembly of the United Nations and serving nine-year terms. It derives its authority from the United Nations Charter, a treaty to which almost all states are party. There is an important difference between a permanent court like the International Court of Justice and the ad hoc arrangements which had previously been normal. Arbitration is a private, essentially contractual arrangement between the states concerned. Its awards have a status in international law that varies according to the quality of its reasoning and its consonance with current conceptions of international law. It may or may not provide some evidence of binding state practice. A permanent court is a more significant mode of adjudication. It is a public body with institutional continuity and institutional authority. Its decisions, unlike those of ad hoc arbitrators, automatically become part of the corpus of international law. So far as they deal with general principles of interstate relations, they are generally a major source of customary international law, binding on states even in the absence of treaty.

The transposition of this model to tribunals adjudicating on the content of domestic law is at first sight rather surprising. Citizens owe allegiance to the state to which they belong. Unlike sovereign states, therefore, they live under a superior authority. States exercise coercive power over their citizens. They have binding internal procedures for imposing their law on those within their territory. This means that the basic problem which makes it necessary to resort to some sort of consensual adjudication on interstate relations does not exist at the domestic level. The blurring of these once clear demarcation lines began in the immediate aftermath of the Second World War. It was provoked by the lessons of the Third Reich. The perception was that the ability of the Third Reich to launch a war of conquest had critically depended on its comprehensive suppression of the personal rights of its own citizens. The Nuremberg Charter imposed criminal liability on individuals, not just on states, for breaches of certain international principles of state conduct. Some of these international principles, like the prohibition of crimes against humanity, operated as rules of domestic conduct overriding domestic law. They applied to acts done by Germans in Germany notwithstanding that they were authorised or even required by German law. The same spirit inspired the United Nations Universal Declaration of Human Rights of 1948, which for the first time laid out a code of rights applying internally to govern the relations between the state and its citizens and, in some respects, the relations of citizens among themselves. The rationale of the Universal Declaration was essentially the same as that of the Nuremberg Charter, namely that 'acts of barbarism' had been committed by the Axis powers in the Second World War whose repetition would be inconsistent with the peace of nations. The legal status of the Universal Declaration is controversial. It is not a treaty but a statement of common aspirations by the nations of the world. Some of its prescriptions may have become part of the corpus of customary international law. The Universal Declaration assumed that adherent states would incorporate its terms into their domestic law, but did not require them to do this and very few have adopted it in its entirety. But it has served as the basis for most international human rights instruments that do create binding obligations. The most notable of these is the International Covenant on Civil and Political Rights. The International Covenant is a treaty sponsored by the United Nations and adopted by the General Assembly in 1966, but it depended for its effect on the adherence of each state. There are currently 167 state parties. They have all accepted an international law obligation as to the contents of their domestic law.

Neither the Universal Declaration nor the International Covenant provided for any tribunal to adjudicate on allegations of breach. But these gaps were filled by a number of regional human rights instruments modelled on them. The earliest and most influential of these was the European Convention on Human Rights, which I will treat as the paradigm case. The European Convention requires signatory states to give effect to it in their domestic law. The European Court of Human Rights, created in 1959, exists to interpret the Convention. Signatory states assume an obligation in international law to abide by the decisions of the Court against them. The Council of Europe enforces this obligation by a process of peer pressure. In practice, states are bound by the decisions of the Court even when they are directed against other states. This is because the Court operates a precedent-based system. If a state ignores a judgment given against another state there will simply be a petition to Strasbourg which will apply the same principle.

Other international tribunals concerned with human rights have proliferated. Most of them are regional, but one notable tribunal with potential worldwide jurisdiction is the International Criminal Court. International tribunals have also proliferated outside the domain of human rights. The most significant of these are the Court of Justice of the European Union, which has recently acquired a human rights jurisdiction in addition to its extensive powers over social and economic policy. There are also more specialised tribunals such as the International Centre for the Settlement of Investment Disputes, part of the World Bank; the World Intellectual Property Organization; and the World Trade Organization Dispute Settlement Body. All of these tribunals depend for their jurisdiction on treaty. What most of them have in common is a claim to determine legal obligations within states and not just between them.

Permanent courts have an important characteristic in common. A good deal of historical experience suggests that new public institutions strive to assert their status and establish a place for themselves in the political firmament. Permanent international tribunals in particular tend to develop a certain institutional *esprit de corps*. With this comes institutional ambitions, a political agenda and a push to enlarge their own jurisdiction at the expense of states. These tendencies are usually restrained in courts like the International Court of Justice, whose interstate jurisdiction is voluntary and advisory. Excessive overreaching would be likely to put off state parties and reduce their influence. Much more problematical are those international tribunals like the European Court of Justice and the European Court of Human Rights, which are endowed by treaty with compulsory jurisdiction. They have no reason to hold back.

Why should any state wish to tie its hands by committing itself to respect the decisions of an international tribunal about its domestic law? The answer is that they do it in what they perceive to be their own long-term interest, even if on occasion they come off worse by the tribunal's decisions. In some cases, this is because the relevant treaty deals with matters that are not amenable to treatment at national level, for example international trade, international insolvency and international transport. This was the main object of the original treaties constituting the European Economic Community and its Court of Justice. The purpose of which was to give member states access to markets extending beyond their own frontiers, something that could be achieved only by international agreement. In other cases, which are becoming increasingly important, states submit to the jurisdiction of international tribunals because they conclude that their interests are best served by adhering to an international rule-based regime extending to their domestic law. The internal legal regimes of states have considerable power to damage the interests of other states. Multilateral treaties ensure a level field. They protect the interest of weaker states against stronger ones, substituting law for power.

The best way of illustrating this point is to examine the conduct of the United States, one of the few states that is economically powerful enough to deal with other countries on its own terms. The United States has generally been reluctant to adhere to international treaties and tribunals that restrict its freedom of action or purport to control the content of its domestic law. When, in 1984, Nicaragua sued the United States in the International Court of Justice for compensation arising from a long course of military and financial interference in its internal affairs, the United States refused to participate and ignored the Court's judgment against it. In 1986, it withdrew from the Court's compulsory jurisdiction and later terminated its acceptance of the Court's jurisdiction over disputes under the Vienna Convention on Consular Relations. The United States has never rejected the notion of a rule-based international order in principle. Indeed it has been the architect of many international codes of law, starting with the Nuremberg Charter. It was the major force behind the Universal Declaration of Human Rights. Its real objection is to the application of these codes to itself. The clearest statement of this notion of American exceptionalism and its relationship to political power was delivered by Hillary Clinton, speaking as a candidate in the Democratic presidential primaries of 2008 in defence of America's reservations about the International Criminal Court. Europe, she said:

> must acknowledge that the United States has global responsibilities that create unique circumstances. For example, we are more vulnerable to the misuse of an international criminal court because of the international role we play and the resentments that flow from that ubiquitous presence around the world ... it is fair to ask that there be sensitivity to those concerns that are really focused on the fact that the United States is active on every continent in the world.

The International Court of Justice and the International Criminal Court operate at the level of international law. But the US position is similar in relation to international tribunals whose decisions directly impact domestic law. The paradigm case is the Dispute Settlement System of the World Trade Organization. With 164 member states representing 98 per cent of global trade, the World Trade Organization supervises a number of treaties seeking to reduce tariffs and non-tariff barriers to trade, such as state aid, export subsidies and unjustified regulatory obstacles. These rules require states to modify their domestic law in areas of economic management once regarded as the essence of sovereignty. Without an international tribunal to enforce them, multilateral trade treaties would be ineffective against the small number of economic superpowers with the market power to set their terms of trade unilaterally. One of those powers is the United States. The United States signed up to the General Agreement on Tariffs and Trade (GATT) and allied treaties because it believed that protectionism was a vice of other states and that the US would benefit from the dismantling of their barriers to US exports. It is no secret that it has been disappointed by the results. Although the US has won many of its disputes before the Settlement Bodies of the WTO, it has also lost some that it did not expect to lose. In February 2020, the Chief US Trade Representative, Mr Robert Lighthizer, presented an angry report to Congress. It is worth quoting his words because the same words could have been directed, in fact frequently have been directed, against other international tribunals such as the European Court of Human Rights and the Court of Justice of the European Union. His report complained that the WTO's Appellate Body had

> added to US obligations and diminished US rights by failing to comply with WTO Rules, addressing issues it has not authority to address, taking actions it has no authority to take, and interpreting WTO agreements in ways not envisioned by the WTO members who entered into those agreements ... There is no legitimacy under our democratic, constitutional system for the nation to submit to a rule imposed by three individuals sitting in

Geneva, with neither agreement by the United States nor approval by the United States Congress. The Appellate Body has consistently acted to increase its own authority while decreasing the authority of the United States and other WTO Members, which, unlike the individuals on the Appellate Body, are accountable to the citizens in their countries – citizens whose lives and livelihoods are affected by the WTO's decisions.

At the time that these words were written, the United States was engaged in a policy of deliberately obstructing the operation of the Settlement Bodies of the WTO. It vetoed all new appointments to the Appellate Body so that eventually there were not enough judges to constitute a dispute panel. This policy attained a high level of rhetorical venom during the presidency of Donald Trump, but it in fact originated under President Obama and has been continued under President Biden. Some other WTO members have reconstituted the Appellate Body by forming an interim appeal body modelled on the WTO's Appellate Body and agreeing to be bound by its decisions. But the United States has effectively removed itself from all processes of independent international trade adjudication. Of course, the price that it has had to pay for this policy is that it can no longer enforce WTO trade treaties against others. But it does not mind, because the stultification of the WTO appeal process has enabled it to get its way by coercion. It has imposed steel tariffs on all its major trading partners and launched a trade war against China, contrary in both cases to its treaty obligations. Only the United States has the will and the economic power to behave in this way. This is a sufficient explanation of why other countries defend the role of international tribunals. There have always been voices calling for European countries to adopt the same approach to international tribunals as the United States. The problem about these suggestions is that in general no European country is strong enough or sufficiently insulated from the vicissitudes of international relations for it to be in its interest to act like the United States. In the area of economic management, the European Union, as the largest international trading block in the world, probably does have that power. It is a great deal less aggressive in using it than the United States. Yet even the European Union has used its economic strength with considerable effect, notably by authorising state subsidies for its aeronautics industries and by imposing on third countries its own rules and the jurisdiction of its own court on competition, data management and international investment agreements, among other subjects. Indeed, the European Union has effectively imposed its rules about data management on the United States companies, as a condition of their being able to operate internationally.

There are populist politicians, in Britain, the United States and elsewhere, who reject international tribunals in principle simply because they are international and for that reason alone intrude upon national sovereignty. This argument is foolish and destructive. Its logical implication is that no state should enter into international treaties, for by definition they all restrict what a sovereign state might otherwise do. But the argument appeals to a particular strand of nationalism that is unwilling to count the cost. The value of international rules depends entirely on whether there are sufficient functional advantages in dealing with the relevant problem at an international level. The United States has generally avoided international jurisdiction, preferring ad hoc arbitrations that it can decline to join or whose judgments it can ignore. This strikes me as profoundly misguided. American exceptionalism will sooner or later create an anti-American world, probably led by China. Short of a return to nineteenth-century-style gunboat diplomacy, friction in international trade and threats to the security of international investment are problems that can only be resolved at international level. We should not forget that the US Smoot–Hawley tariffs played a significant supporting role in the destabilisation of the world economy and the rise of aggressive totalitarianism in Europe in the 1930s, as well as damaging major US export industries when other countries retaliated. Nor should we forget that the United States has for many years been among the world's largest exporters of capital and has more at risk than any country from the threat of expropriation or discrimination by other autarkic regimes.

It is, however, important to distinguish between matters that are best addressed at the international level, and those that states can handle perfectly effectively at an exclusively national level. Treaties regulating international trade and economic cooperation impede the free exercise of national sovereignty, but they may also confer considerable benefits which few states can achieve on their own. The classic example is perhaps the European Union, in which the subordination of national sovereignty is the price paid for a prize of immense value, namely the creation of a single market of half a billion consumers. Human rights treaties are different. There is nothing in the Universal Declaration on Human Rights or the International Covenant on Civil and Political Rights or the European Human Rights Convention that cannot be achieved by ordinary domestic legislation if there is sufficient democratic support for it. Many of the questions addressed by international human rights treaties have been addressed at the national level for centuries. In Britain the more important rights that we now classify as human rights were recognised as part of the common law by the great jurist Blackstone in the eighteenth century. Others were adopted by statute or judicial decision long before Britain incorporated the Convention into its domestic law in 1998.

The question therefore arises what is the benefit to any state of dealing with human rights by international treaty.

When the European Convention on Human Rights was originally drafted in 1950 it could reasonably be regarded as part of the normal pattern of multilateral treaties. Ever since the seventeenth century, the history of Europe had shown a direct relationship between domestic authoritarianism and international aggression. The Convention was conceived to be in the common interest of western Europe in order to prevent the rise of new despotisms of the kind that had disturbed the peace of Europe from Louis XIV and Napoleon to Adolf Hitler and Vladimir Putin. This ambition is reflected in its fourth recital, which declares that it was the 'profound belief' of the adherents that the rights and freedoms contained in it were 'the foundation of justice and peace in the world and are best maintained on the one hand by an effective political democracy and on the other by a common understanding and observance of the Human Rights upon which they depend'. This view was particularly strongly held by the United Kingdom, which had played a prominent part in the negotiation of the Convention. It was a catalogue of values which the Third Reich had violated and which the Soviet Union and the governments under its control in eastern Europe were still violating. The United Kingdom took the view that the Convention protected rights which had for many years been embodied in its own domestic law, but needed to be exported to other less fortunate and potentially more dangerous states. On that footing it had genuine functional advantages that could only be addressed at the international level.

This benign view of the European Convention has been rudely disturbed by the growing activism of the European Court of Human Rights. The Strasbourg Court is the clearest example of the tendency of permanent international tribunals with compulsory jurisdiction to enlarge it and to acquire a political agenda. Whole books could be written, indeed have been written, to illustrate this development. Three examples may be cited. They are probably the most significant.

The first is the Court's expansion of its geographical reach. Article 1 of the Convention obliged the contracting parties to secure the specified rights and freedoms on 'everyone within their jurisdiction'. That clearly means its territorial jurisdiction, in accordance with the principle of territoriality in international law. In 2001, the Court was invited to apply the Convention to the participation by European states in NATO's bombing of Belgrade. It refused to do so on the ground that the Convention was not designed or suitable for conditions in non-Convention countries. Then, without any explanation, the Court abruptly reversed its position in 2011 and gave a series of judgments on UN-sponsored peacekeeping operations in Iraq and Afghanistan. Some of these decisions have treated the European Human Rights Convention as prevailing over the Charter of the United Nations. Others have hamstrung European armies engaged in UN-sponsored peacekeeping operations, for example by restricting their right to hold Taliban fighters as prisoners of war after they had been captured in battle. This has caused dismay not only in European defence ministries but at the United Nations and in the International Red Cross. It is one of the worst and most damaging developments in Strasbourg's history.

Secondly, in *Soering v United Kingdom* in 1989, the Court imposed on member states of the Council of Europe the duty in certain circumstances to apply the Convention to the practices of non-Convention states. In *Soering* itself, the United Kingdom was prevented from extraditing an alleged murderer to Virginia unless the United States undertook that he would not be sentenced to death in accordance with Virginia's criminal code.

Thirdly, the Strasbourg Court has greatly expanded the scope of Article 8 of the Convention, which protects private and family life. This article was designed to protect against the surveillance state in totalitarian regimes. But the Court has developed it into what it calls a 'principle of personal autonomy'. Acting on this principle, it has extended Article 8 so that it potentially covers anything that affects an individual's person's autonomous development. It is obvious that most laws seek to do that to some degree. They impose standards of behaviour that people would not necessarily adopt voluntarily. This may be illustrated by the vast range of issues that the Strasbourg Court has held to be covered by Article 8. They include the legal status of illegitimate children, immigration and deportation, extradition, criminal sentencing, the recording of crime, abortion, artificial insemination, homosexuality and same sex unions, child abduction, the policing of public demonstrations, employment and social security rights, legal aid, planning and environmental law, noise abatement, eviction for non-payment of rent, and much else besides. All of these things have been included in the protection of private and family life without any warrant in the language of the Convention.

The ordinary principles of international law governing the interpretation of treaties are codified by the Vienna Convention on the Law of Treaties. Article 31 of that Convention provides that a treaty 'shall be interpreted in good faith in accordance with the ordinary meaning to be given to the terms of the treaty in their context and in the light of its object and purpose'. This reflects a principle that is even more important as applied to international treaties than to domestic legal instruments. The parties to treaties are sovereign states who are entitled to decide for themselves what international obligations to accept. The text is the only thing that they can realistically be said to have agreed. It is therefore the starting point and the finishing point. The surrounding circumstances may be used to elucidate the meaning of the text, but not to modify it. The approach of the Strasbourg Court has been very different. It has effectively emancipated itself from the text. Its judgments have transformed the Convention from a protection against domestic despotism into a template for most aspects of human life. The principle behind these changes has been summed up in the phrase 'living instrument', which was first articulated in the Court's decision in *Tyrer v United Kingdom* in 1978. The phrase refers to the process by which the Court develops the Convention by way of extrapolation or analogy, so as to reflect its own view of what additional rights a modern democracy ought to have. The European Human Rights Convention has become what on other occasions I have called a dynamic treaty, that is to say it not only lays down the obligations that states have agreed to be bound by, but contains a supranational mechanism for developing and expanding those obligations independently of the decision of the state parties. The Strasbourg Court issues more than 4,000 judgments a year, with a backlog in 2022 of some 75,000 applications. It has become much more than a judicial body. It is a great factory for making law, which has become a legislative and political authority for the whole of Europe. It is legislative because it claims and exercises the power to require state parties to modify their domestic law in accordance with its own views about what kind of laws a democracy ought to have. It is political because many of the issues that it decides are matters of political judgment on which states and indeed their citizens can legitimately differ.

Public opinion has by and large accepted these changes in the role of the European Court of Human Rights. In Britain, polling evidence consistently shows majorities against withdrawing from the European Convention. Their views generally depend on whether they agree with those decisions that they are aware of. Except perhaps in the context of immigration and penal policy, they generally do agree, because the Strasbourg Court's decisions usually have the effect of diminishing the authority of the state. People are much less concerned with the constitutional implications of making decisions about the content of domestic law in this way. Britain has a litigious culture, more so than any other European country. People welcome any avenue of appeal, especially against the state. Yet the constitutional implications of submitting to an international tribunal on the contents of domestic law are more problematic than people realise. The recognition of rights is not a cost-free option. It imposes obligations which represent a burden on society. This is entirely acceptable in a democracy, where we choose our burdens. The state represents us, or can be made to do so by ordinary political processes. Domestic judicial intervention can be regulated by domestic laws. But there is no such justification for curtailing the action of the state by international jurisdictions. Democratic majorities have no influence into the lawmaking processes of the Strasbourg Court, and no way of amending the law that the Strasbourg Court imposes.

The effect of the 'living instrument' doctrine is to transfer an essentially legislative power to an international body standing outside the constitutional framework of the United Kingdom and outside the collective mechanisms by which we consent to the laws that govern us. What lies behind this is a profound distrust of democratic decision-making because of its potentially illiberal implications. The purpose, and certainly the effect of international human rights law as it currently stands, is to replace domestic law (into which democratic electorates have some input) by international law (into which they have none at all) as the main source of law in important areas of our national life. Judges, whether national or international, exist to apply the law. It is the business of citizens and their representatives to decide what the law ought to be. In a democracy, the appropriate way of resolving what the law ought to be is through the political process. The only alternative to a political resolution of our differences is to invite the judges to legislate. International human rights tribunals such as the Strasbourg Court are intensely ideological bodies which do this too readily. They legislate in a way that bypasses political consent and is practically incapable of modification or amendment. They transform controversial political issues into questions of law for the courts. In this way, they take critical decision-making powers out of the political process. Since that process is the only method by which the population at large is able to engage, however indirectly, in the shaping of law, this is hard to justify.

Perhaps the most problematic area of Strasbourg jurisprudence concerns qualified Convention rights. These are rights which the Convention says may be subject to exceptions where this is 'necessary in a democratic society' because of some sufficiently important countervailing public interest. Examples of countervailing public interests include national security, public order, the prevention of disease and the economic well-being of society. Most Convention rights are qualified in this way, and most disputes are about the qualifications. Yet who is to judge what countervailing public interests are sufficiently important or what is necessary in a democratic society? Balancing competing public interests is the essence of democratic government and participatory politics. How much privacy are we prepared to sacrifice in the interests of efficient policing? How much liberty are we prepared to sacrifice in the interests of preventing the spread of disease? How much freedom of speech are we prepared to sacrifice in the interests of ethnic harmony or the protection of personal reputation? These are intensely political questions. Not every society will answer them in the same way. But the Strasbourg Court has classified them as questions of law for judges. It has arrogated to itself the right to decide between competing public interests, and to determine what is necessary in a democratic society, irrespective of the views of democratic electorates.

International human rights tribunals inevitably treat human societies as if they were the same when manifestly they are not. They are bound to do this, because the principle that underlies modern human rights theory is that there are some inalienable rights which human beings enjoy, not by the largesse of the state or the forbearance of their fellow citizens but because they are inherent in their humanity. Yet this principle has always been problematic. Rights are the creation of law. Laws are, among other things, an expression of the collective values of the society that makes them and not of humanity at large. Humanity is not a uniform product like rice grains or wood chips. Different societies have their own political traditions, their own social conventions, their own moral and religious values and their own physical conditions. Moreover, the relations between a state and its citizens do not simply depend on law. They are highly sensitive to its legal, social and political culture, which are the product of its history. Much depends on the strength of a country's political and administrative system. To take an obvious example, the practical problems of constraining the state are not the same in a country recently released from centuries of autocratic government as they are in a country with robust traditions, a developed system of public law and an independent judiciary. Nations do not all have the same basic legal needs or priorities, and should not necessarily be expected to confer the same rights.

These complaints about the Strasbourg Court may sound very like Mr Robert Lighthizer's complaints about the Appellate Body of the World Trade Organization. But there are two important differences. One is that when one examines them, most of the complaints of the US Trade Representative about the decisions of the Appellate Body of the WTO were simply based on the fact that he disagreed with the result. He thought that the United States should have won. Like all tribunals, international tribunals may get the law wrong. It does not follow that they have exceeded their jurisdiction as Mr Lighthizer suggested. His accusation against the WTO's settlement system is a good deal less plausible than the corresponding accusation against the Strasbourg Court, whose living instrument doctrine overtly asserts a right to revise the Convention in accordance with wider values of its own. The second and perhaps more important difference is that world trade friction can only be dealt with internationally, whereas human rights can be dealt with at a purely domestic level. By expanding its reach to cover most aspects of domestic law, the Strasbourg Court has single-handedly undermined the sole justification for dealing with these matters at the international level. The wholesale abandonment of basic civil rights by significant nations remains a threat to world peace and to international relations generally, as the Russian invasion of Ukraine has shown. The same cannot be said about the rules governing noise abatement, the conduct of inquests, in vitro fertilisation and many other matters with which the Strasbourg Court has gratuitously interfered.

The extent of the Strasbourg Court's ambition to become an international legislature has recently been starkly demonstrated by the remarkable decision of the Grand Chamber on climate change: *Verein Klimaseniorinnen Schweiz v Switzerland* (9 April 2024). The facts were that the Swiss constitution requires any enactment of the Swiss parliament to be put to a confirmatory referendum if a minimum number of citizens call for one. In 2021 the Swiss electorate rejected in a referendum an Act of the Swiss Parliament requiring a 30 per cent reduction in emissions from 1990 levels by 2030. So in the following year it was replaced by a more moderate Act providing for a staged reduction to net zero by 2050 (the same as the current statutory target in the UK). The Swiss approved the new Act in a referendum in 2022. There is nothing in the Human Rights Convention requiring any particular standard of public health protection and there is certainly nothing about climate change. But Article 8 entitles any citizen to 'respect for his private and family life, his home and his correspondence'. The Strasbourg Court held that this implied a right to require governments to take 'effective measures' to protect the health of the population against climate change. By 'effective measures' the Court meant measures consistent with the views of the UN Intergovernmental Panel on Climate Change. By that standard Swiss law was found wanting. Something like the statute that they rejected was needed. Rejecting the referendum result as irrelevant, the Court observed that 'democracy cannot be reduced to the will of the majority of the electorate and elected representatives, in disregard of the requirements of the rule of law'. Few decisions have so openly expressed the Strasbourg Court's contempt for democracy or claimed for its judges a roving brief covering the whole field of national public policy. By any reasonable intellectual standard, the right to respect for private and family life, the home and correspondence does not imply any rule governing climate change policy.

The decision in the climate change case is problematic for a number of other reasons.

In the first place, it represents a highly autocratic approach to a major issue of policy. The question is not whether the Strasbourg Court is right about climate change, but how we should make law on such an issue in a democracy. The appropriate rate of emissions reduction, the timescale over which it is to be achieved, the desirability and feasibility of net zero targets, the allowance to be made for physical conditions in different parts of the world, and the share of the burden to be assumed by industrialised countries are all intensely controversial questions. The Swiss like other states of the Council of Europe are entitled to a consensual process for resolving these differences in accordance with their constitution. That is what the rule of law means. The Court expressly acknowledged that it was not competent to replace national governments and legislatures, but that is exactly what it has purported to do. It has declared that the rule of law requires the forty-six member states of the Council of Europe to accept its ruling as law, overriding their own democratic procedures. In the case of Switzerland, this appears to mean not just that Switzerland must change its statute law, but also that it must change its constitution so as to prevent citizens from rejecting the change in a referendum.

Secondly, the Strasbourg Court's decision illustrates the practical problems about the judicial creation of positive rights. It is an irresponsible way to make very bad law. Climate change is a classic polycentric issue. There is an urgent need for measures to address it. But governments cannot sensibly consider it in isolation from other relevant factors. They have to take into account the impact on whole populations who have built their lives on past assumptions about the availability of energy. People need to heat their homes, get to work, run businesses and so on. Many live on very tight budgets. There is a trade-off between these competing policy imperatives. Difficult compromises may be required. Yet the Strasbourg Court considered nothing but climate change. That is how courts work. They address the particular issue put before them by the complainant. They do not look at the collateral issues raised by most demands for the enactment of positive rights. Responsible states cannot make major decisions affecting peoples' lives on such a blinkered basis.

Thirdly, the Strasbourg Court's inventive approach to the interpretation of the Convention is difficult to reconcile with the rule of law. As I have previously observed, the first requirement of the rule of law is that the law should be such that people can be guided by it. In other words, it must be stable, publicly accessible, clear and not retrospective. It is not consistent with these principles for a court to devise new rights, previously unrecognised and not foreshadowed in the text, simply because it considers that they are desirable, and then to apply them retrospectively as if they had always been obvious.

For many years I believed that the Strasbourg Court could be reformed and that it was right to remain a member of the Council of Europe in the hope that this would happen. But I had concluded even before the climate change case that reform was no longer feasible. A previous attempt to moderate the inventive zeal of the Court, through the Brighton Declaration of 2012, has failed. The Court is dominated by its president and a handful of powerful chamber chairs. It has a legal staff of some two hundred strongly ideological lawyers who do most of the drafting and have a great deal of influence over the Court's decisions and reasoning. I believe that Britain should withdraw from the Convention, but incorporate its text into its statute law, adding such additional protections as seem desirable. This would enable us to defend all the same basic rights without submitting to the overbearing regulatory instincts of the Strasbourg Court. Other countries with judicial systems similar to Britain's, such as Canada and New Zealand, have a high reputation for defending human rights without submitting their domestic arrangements to the scrutiny of an international court. In a country such as the United Kingdom, with independent and apolitical courts of high standing, it is unnecessary to have another tier of judicial supervision at the international level.

Although the Convention system has changed beyond recognition in the six decades since the Strasbourg Court opened for business, in Britain the debate over its role has hardly advanced at all. It is usually conducted on the assumption that if Britain were to withdraw from the Convention there would be no domestic protection for human rights. But that would depend on what was enacted to replace the Convention. No one, so far as I am aware, has suggested, and I certainly do not suggest, that nothing should replace it. Defenders of the Convention system rarely address its implications for our constitution and our domestic law. Most of them defend it on the same ground as the original drafters, as if nothing had changed, i.e. as an instrument of British foreign policy. The argument is that more benighted countries need Britain's example to keep them on the path of civilisation, that our withdrawal might encourage others to follow suit, and that without the Convention Britain would become an international pariah. None of these arguments are realistic. There may well be other states tempted to withdraw from the Convention, but if they do it will be because of their own domestic problems with Strasbourg, and not because Britain has done so. Those countries that want a code of human rights are unlikely to be discouraged from having one by Britain's decision to nationalise its own code, while the autocratic governments that have suppressed basic civil rights in their own countries have plainly been unmoved by Britain's example.

In most Western countries, domestic political institutions have suffered a grave loss of authority and prestige, which has opened the door to the kind of international judicial legislation that I have been discussing. This tendency is likely to persist as unrealistic or disappointed expectations of democracy mount. There is much to be said for a rule-based international order in areas where international cooperation is necessary. But the tolerance of democratic electorates will wear thin if it continues to overreach itself by internationalising issues of domestic policy. Immigration is already proving to be a flashpoint, not just in Britain but in other European countries. The risk is that populists exploiting discontent over the remoteness of decision-making will repudiate the whole international order, good, bad and indifferent, to substitute something worse: a world of disruptive international relations and competitive autocracies.

X

MISSION CREEP: ARTICLE 6 OF THE HUMAN RIGHTS CONVENTION*

For some years I have expressed concern about the expanding claims of the European Court of Human Rights in Strasbourg to jurisdiction over Britain's domestic legal order. Criticisms of the Court tend to focus on its remarkably expansive interpretation of Article 8, which protects private and family life, but has been extended to cover most aspects of human well-being. In this chapter, I propose to illustrate my concerns by reference to another article of the Convention: Article 6. Article 6 provides that 'in the determination of his civil rights and obligations, or of any criminal charge against him, everyone is entitled to a fair and public hearing within a reasonable time by an independent and impartial tribunal established by law'. The language is simple enough. Yet it has been the most fertile source of petitions to the European Court of Human Rights, and has accounted for the largest number of violations. Between 1959 and 2022, over a quarter of all violations found by the Court were violations of Article 6. The principal offenders were Turkey and the countries of the old communist block, notably Russia and Romania. The United Kingdom is well down the list of

---

* This is an updated version of the James Wood Lecture given at the University of Glasgow in November 2015.

offenders, but it has had its own collisions with Article 6. In the same period there were 97 cases in which the Strasbourg Court found violations of Article 6 by the United Kingdom, more than any other article. In addition, since the Human Rights Act came into force in 2000, the United Kingdom courts have on three occasions made declarations of incompatibility based on Article 6.

Numbers, of course, do not tell the whole story. In addition to cases in which the United Kingdom has been found to have violated Article 6, there has been a fair number of cases since 2000 in which a violation of the article has only been avoided by applying the muscular principles of interpretation required by section 3 of the Human Rights Act, or by quashing subordinate legislation or other executive acts. More generally, Article 6 has had a significant influence on criminal procedure and on new legislation, notably in the fields of criminal sentencing and penal policy and in the creation of fresh avenues of review of administrative decisions. So we may take it that although our violations of Article 6 are neither as frequent nor as serious as those of Russia, Romania or Turkey, the article raises significant issues for the United Kingdom.

I shall focus on one particular aspect of Article 6, namely what has been called the 'right to a court'. This is the right, which has been held to be implicit in Article 6, not just to have legal proceedings fairly conducted but to bring legal proceedings at all, and to do so without having to confront some legal, administrative or practical obstacle. This principle provides an interesting and revealing case study of the way in which the jurisprudence of the European Court of Human Rights tends to expand the scope of the Convention.

The origin of the 'right to a court' is the decision of the Strasbourg Court in *Golder v United Kingdom* (1979–80) 1 EHRR 524. The facts were simple enough. Mr Golder was a prisoner serving a fifteen-year sentence for robbery with violence at Parkhurst prison in the Isle of Wight. A prison officer had written an entry in his prison record alleging that he had participated in a serious riot. As a result, he had suffered two weeks in solitary confinement and was at risk of being refused parole at the end of his sentence. He denied that he had had anything to do with the riot, and proposed to instruct a solicitor to sue the prison officer for libel. But under Rule 33 of the Prison Regulations as they then stood, a prisoner was not allowed to communicate with any outsider in connection with any legal business without the permission of the Home Secretary, which in this instance was refused. So in 1970, Mr Golder petitioned the Strasbourg Court.

Mr Golder's petition worked its way through the Strasbourg process at a critical stage in its history. The Court had very little business in the early 1970s. People were not as conscious of the Convention as they later became. Its jurisdiction to hear individual petitions was limited to states that had opted to allow them. The United Kingdom had only recently exercised that option, and many states had still not done so. The decision to allow individual petitions from the United Kingdom had been made by the Labour government in 1966. They made it partly because they believed that it would make little difference. They assumed that the Strasbourg institutions could be expected to respect the limits of what the Convention states had actually agreed. By the early 1970s, however, with a Conservative government in power, the picture had begun to look very different. Under the procedure which then obtained, petitions were dealt with in the first instance by the European Commission on Human Rights. They did not reach the Court unless the Commission or a Convention state referred the case to them. In the view of the UK government, the Commission had shown a distressing tendency to expand the scope of the Convention by implying additional rights into it that had not been agreed by the Convention states. An important milestone was passed in October 1970, when the Commission ruled that 243 applications by East African Asians who had been refused a right of entry into the UK were admissible on the ground that Article 3, which prohibits inhuman or degrading treatment, was capable of applying to acts of racial discrimination. Lord Lester of Herne Hill, who as Anthony Lester QC was counsel for the applicants, naturally welcomed the decision, but he is on record as saying that he had originally doubted whether the Court would be so bold.

In March 1971, six months after the admissibility decision in the East African Asians case, the Commission declared Mr Golder's complaint to be admissible, and in their report on the merits in June 1973, they upheld it. They held that the right to a fair trial implied a right to a trial. It was therefore violated by any administrative measure that restricted a person's right to instruct a solicitor. The British government referred the case to the Court. They were not especially concerned about the particular position of Mr Golder. The Parole Board had not in fact been told about the prison officer's accusation, and he had been released without difficulty more than a year before the Commission reported. The government was much more concerned about the Commission's propensity to add implied rights to the Convention. They wanted to treat Mr Golder's complaint as a test case on the general approach to the interpretation of the Convention. Thus it was that Mr Golder found himself in Strasbourg up against the combined learning of two former legal advisers to the Foreign Office, Professor Sir Francis Vallat KCMG, QC, and Sir William Dale KCMG, and Mr Gordon Slynn QC, the future Lord Slynn of Hadley. The argument of these great luminaries was that the Convention was not designed to protect all human rights. It was intended to protect only those particular rights upon which the parties to the original Convention had been able to agree upon when it was drafted in 1950. There was therefore, in their submission, no justification for extending the scope of the Convention any further than its language warranted. The Foreign Office obviously shared Mr Lester's view that they would get a more cautious approach from the Court than from the Commission.

As it turned out, they were both wrong. The Court adopted the Commission's line, and *Golder* became one of the leading cases on the teleological approach to the application of the Convention. The Court held that there was a right to put a civil dispute before a court, and not just a right to have it tried fairly when it got there. Their reasoning was based on the rule of law. They began by drawing attention to Article 31 of the Vienna Convention on the Interpretation of Treaties, which authorises resort to general principles of law recognised by civilised countries as an aid to interpretation. The rule of law was such a principle. Starting from this position, they reasoned as follows: Article 6, by requiring civil disputes to be determined at a fair and public hearing before an independent and impartial tribunal, was designed to give effect to the rule of law – the rule of law also required a right of access to the courts – therefore Article 6 must also be taken to require a right of access to a court. They reinforced this conclusion by a *reductio ad absurdum*. If there was no right to a court, the right to a fair and public hearing before an impartial and independent tribunal was not worth much. A state would always be able to 'do away with its courts, or take away their jurisdiction to determine certain classes of civil actions and entrust it to organs dependent on the Government'.

There were three dissenting judgments. The longest and most acrimonious of them came from the British judge, Sir Gerald Fitzmaurice, a notable international lawyer and himself a former Legal Adviser to the Foreign Office, who had worked on the drafting of the Convention while it was being negotiated. His dissent is worth studying, because it goes to the heart of the difference between the supporters and the opponents of the Strasbourg's Court's expansive approach to the Convention. The difference between the Commission and the UK government, he observed, was not really about the meaning of the Convention. The rival arguments represented different juridical frames of mind. The UK government submitted that Article 1 bound the state parties to give effect to the rights 'defined' in the following articles, and no right to a court was defined in Article 6. The argument of the Commission, on the other hand,

> amounted to this – that it is inconceivable, or at least inadmissible, that a convention on human rights should fail in some form or other to provide for a right of access to the courts: therefore it must be presumed to do so if such an inference is at all possible from any of its terms.

This approach, he said, might be legitimate from a legislator, but not from a court of law. There was, he said,

> a considerable difference between the case of 'law-giver's law' edicted in the exercise of sovereign power, and law based on convention, itself the outcome of a process of agreement, and limited to what has been agreed, or can properly be assumed to have been agreed. Far greater interpretational restraint is requisite in the latter case, in which, accordingly, the Convention should not be construed as providing for more than it contains, or than is necessarily to be inferred from what it contains.

The Court's approach, according to Fitzmaurice, was

typical of the cry of the judicial legislator all down the ages – a cry which, whatever justification it may have on the internal or national plane, has little or none in the domain of the inter-State treaty or Convention based on agreement and governed by that essential fact ... The point is that it is for the States upon whose consent the Convention rests, and from which consent alone it derives its obligatory force, to close the gap or put the defect right by an amendment, not for a judicial tribu-nal to substitute itself for the Convention-makers, to do their work for them.

Whether or not one agrees with Sir Gerald Fitzmaurice's interpretation of Article 6, he put his finger on the real differ-ence between the two sides of the argument. He also correctly identified the wider significance of the majority's judgment. The decision in *Golder* marked, at an early stage of the Court's history, its adoption of an approach to the inter-pretation of the Convention that was radically different from the approach of international tribunals to the interpretation of treaties generally. Instead of seeking to ascertain the intentions of the contracting parties from the language, the preparatory papers (*travaux*) and other recognised aids to interpretation, the articles of the Convention were in effect to be treated as a body of legal principle capable of autono-mous legal development in accordance with the values that its provisions might be said to represent. This is essentially a process of extrapolation rather than interpretation. It is more like the way that the common law develops autono-mously into new areas. The expression 'living instrument' was not coined until three years later. But the concept was adopted in *Golder* well before the phrase was devised in *Tyrer v United Kingdom* (1979–80) 2 EHRR 1. The potential for expanding the scope of the Convention into new areas was at least one reason for the exponential growth of the Strasbourg Court's business, which began in the late 1970s. *Golder* was the first judgment of the Court to which Sir Gerald Fitzmaurice was party. He became a persistent critic of the Court, and dissented in most of the eleven cases on which he sat during his time as one of its judges.

I have no difficulty with the actual result in *Golder*. I think that it *is* implicit in a rule that civil rights and obligations will be determined at a fair and public hearing before an independent and impartial tribunal, that a litigant will be allowed access to that tribunal in order to determine his claim. The proposition seems to me to be no more radical than the corresponding common-law rule which the courts have repeatedly recognised over the past half-century. As early as the 1760s, Blackstone wrote in his *Commentaries* (4th edition, 1876, III):

> A ... right of every [man] is that of applying to the courts of justice for redress of injuries. Since the law is in England the supreme arbiter of every man's life, liberty and property, courts of justice must at all times be open to the subject and the law be duly administered therein.

Indeed, the French text of Article 6 comes very close to saying this in terms (*Toute personne a le droit à ce que sa cause soit entendue équitablement*). The problem about *Golder* lies not in the result, which is unexceptionable, but in the reasoning. In basing its judgment mainly on the rule of law, the Strasbourg Court raised a major question that it left unanswered, namely what does the rule of law require in this context.

Golder was a very simple case. If the officer's report about Mr Golder was untrue, as Mr Golder alleged, then he had a good cause of action for libel. It was common ground that the English courts would have received and determined his action whether or not his instructions to his solicitor had been communicated in breach of the Prison Regulations. So the real effect of the Prison Regulations was to confer a discretionary administrative power on the Home Secretary to obstruct the exercise of a legal right, by preventing Mr Golder from invoking the jurisdiction of the courts. Moreover, in this instance, the power had been exercised so as to prevent Mr Golder from suing an employee of the Prison Service itself. This was manifestly an interference with Mr Golder's right to a fair hearing. Equally, once one accepts that there may be a right not to be obstructed from accessing the Court, it is a short step to holding that in some cases the state may be obliged to provide positive assistance, for example by way of legal aid, in a case where without it a litigant will be unable to exercise his rights. This was the step that the Strasbourg Court took in 1979 in *Airey v Ireland* (1979–80) 2 EHRR 305.

The principle accepted in *Golder* and again in *Airey* has, however, been treated as decisive of many cases in which the petitioner's problem did not arise from any difficulty in accessing the Court, but from the rules of law that fell to be applied when he got there. This can happen in a number of ways. The courts may lack jurisdiction under their own law. Or there may be a procedural bar, such as the expiry of a limitation period. Or the claimant may simply have no legal right to assert under the domestic law. These are all examples of legal rules that, without preventing access to a court, may prevent a civil claim from succeeding. Such rules are law, and on the face of it the rule of law requires that effect should be given to them. On that footing, there is only one basis on which Article 6 could be relevant. That is that the article is not just concerned with removing obstacles in the way of a litigant seeking to enforce their legal rights. It also determines what limits may properly be placed upon the scope of those rights. It therefore has potential implications for the substantive law of every Convention state.

One answer to these questions might have been that Article 6 is not about the content of the domestic law of Convention states governing liability. It is only about procedure. When the Duke of Westminster complained, in *James v United Kingdom* (1986) 8 EHRR 123, that the Leasehold Reform Act 1967 allowed his qualifying leaseholders to compulsorily purchase his freeholds without providing any grounds on which he could object before a court, he was met with the answer (para. 81) that Article 6 'does not in itself guarantee any particular content for (civil) rights and obligations in the substantive law of the Contracting States'. In *Fayed v United Kingdom* (1994) 18 EHRR 393, the Court expanded this statement. 'The Court,' it said, 'may not create through the interpretation of Article 6 § 1 a substantive right which has no legal basis in the State concerned'. These formulae have been repeated time and again in the subsequent case law of the Strasbourg Court. But, as so often in Strasbourg, these forthright statements do not quite mean what they seem to say. Article 6 has been the vehicle for some quite striking incursions into the substantive content of domestic law.

The two landmark cases were *Ashingdane v United Kingdom* (1985) 7 EHRR 528 and *Fayed v United Kingdom* (1994) 18 EHRR 393. In both of these cases, petitions based on Article 6 failed, but the reasoning considerably extended the scope of the article to cover the content of the domestic rules of law.

Ashingdane arose out of the Mental Health Act 1959, which conferred extensive powers on public authorities to commit mental patients to hospitals. Section 141 of the Act provided that no one should be civilly liable for anything done pursuant to the Act unless it was done in bad faith or negligently. Mr Ashingdane had been detained under the Act in a secure facility, Broadmoor Hospital, on the grounds that he was a dangerous schizophrenic. After a certain amount of time, it was decided that he could safely be transferred to a less secure establishment. But he remained in Broadmoor because no other psychiatric hospital could be found to accept him. He sued the Department of Health for breach of statutory duty in failing to transfer him, but found his action barred by section 141. On the face of it, here was a statutory rule that determined the content of Mr Ashingdane's civil rights against the health authorities. In the absence of bad faith or negligence he had no claim against them under English law. The Court of Appeal struck out the claim. They held that the alleged breach of statutory duty was not based on either bad faith or absence of reasonable care, and that was the end of the matter. The Strasbourg Court accepted that Mr Ashingdane had been able to go before the courts, even if the outcome was that his action failed. But that, they said, was not the end of the matter. 'It must still be established that the degree of access afforded under the national legislation was sufficient to secure the individual's "right to a court", having regard to the rule of law in a democratic society' (para. 57). That, they said, required the Court to decide whether section 141 pursued a legitimate objective and to apply a proportionality test. In particular the Court had to be satisfied that the statute did not impair the essence of Mr Ashingdane's rights. As it happened, section 141 was held to be both legitimate in principle and proportionate as applied to Mr Ashingdane. By inference the Strasbourg Court must also have thought that it did not impair the essence of his right. But the startling result of the Court's reasoning was that an applicant's right to a court might be interfered with simply because under the law of England he had no cause of action. Moreover, because the proportionality of applying section 141 had to be decided in the light of the particular impact that that would have on Mr Ashingdane, the Strasbourg Court appeared to be saying that rules of substantive law which applied to particular categories of person had to be applied on a discretionary basis.

Nearly a decade later, the Strasbourg Court had to deal with the case of *Fayed v United Kingdom* (1994) 18 EHRR 393. The late Mohamed Fayed was a notable friend of the legal profession who probably needs no introduction. Inspectors appointed under the Companies Acts had published a report in which they made serious criticisms of his honesty. His complaint was that he could not sue them successfully for libel because they were entitled to qualified privilege. Qualified privilege is the principle that you cannot recover damages for defamation from a person who is acting under a duty, unless he acted maliciously. Mr Fayed had not been deprived of access to the Court any more than Mr Ashingdane had. His problem was that since the facts did not warrant a plea of malice, his claim was bound to fail. Qualified privilege is a rule of substantive law. Where it applies, it is a defence to liability. But the Strasbourg Court declined to decide what sort of rule it was. They held that whether it was a procedural bar or a rule of substantive law, Article 6 required it to be reviewed for legitimacy and proportionality. They must therefore have thought that by allowing a defence of privilege to a libel claimant, English law was restricting Mr Fayed's right to a court in a manner that needed to be justified. Their reason for taking this view seems to have been that they regarded a defence such as qualified privilege, which is available only to a defendant acting under a duty, as a personal immunity. Thus they held that it would be inconsistent with the rule of law if the state were to 'confer immunities from civil liability on large groups or categories of persons'.

This seems most surprising. Before one can regard a legal rule as conferring an immunity on a person, one has to be satisfied that it relieves him of a liability that he would otherwise have been under. What liabilities he would otherwise have been under must depend not just on the elements of legal liability but on the availability of any legal defences. The approach of the Strasbourg Court in *Fayed* seems to have been that a defence such as qualified privilege, which was available only to some categories of persons, must for that reason alone be regarded as an immunity. However, as a general statement, that simply cannot be right. Whether a defence amounts to an immunity must depend, surely, on the reason why the defence exists. Very few legal liabilities are unqualified. Most qualifications reflect some reservation about the kind of activities that ought to give rise to liability. The defence of qualified privilege is broadly speaking available in cases where the law regards the activity in which the defendant was engaged as giving rise to a duty in whose performance there is a public interest. That duty may authorise them to say unkind things about other people, provided that they do so without malice. There is a world of difference between a defence of this kind and an immunity based on status. If Article 6 can nullify a defence in this way, it is in effect turning a qualified liability into an unqualified one. The effect is to create through the interpretation of Article 6 a substantive right that has no basis in the law of the state concerned, precisely the exercise that the Court in *Fayed* acknowledged to be illegitimate.

The muddle that the Strasbourg Court got into on this question was cruelly exposed by its decision in *Osman v United Kingdom* (2000) 29 EHRR 245. Mr Osman had been killed by a man who was subsequently convicted of manslaughter by reason of diminished responsibility. His widow and son sued the police for negligence in failing to act on evidence of the killer's aberrant behaviour in the period before he struck. English, like Scottish law, recognises a duty of care as existing only if certain conditions are satisfied. One of them is that it should satisfy the public policy test, i.e. that it is fair, just and reasonable that such a duty should be owed. In *Hill v Chief Constable of West Yorkshire* (1989) AC 53, the House of Lords had held that, absent a specific assumption of responsibility, it was not fair, just and reasonable that a duty of care should be owed by the police to the public in relation to the investigation or prevention of crime. As a result, the Osmans' action was struck out as unarguable in the High Court. This was held by the Strasbourg Court to be a violation of Article 6. There is no doubt that the Strasbourg Court misunderstood some aspects of the English law of tort. In particular it did not appreciate that the decision in *Hill* had been about the sorts of activity that could give rise to a duty of care as a matter of law. They assumed that the question whether it was fair, just and reasonable to impose liability had to be decided on a case-by-case basis in the light of the particular facts, and that the English court had been prevented from carrying out that exercise by the order striking out the claim. However, the main reason why the Court found a violation of Article 6 was a different one. They made the same mistake as the Court had made in *Fayed*. They treated the non-liability of the police as a kind of institutional immunity based on status, and concluded that it was too broad to be proportionate. Actually, the law was that the police owed no duty to the Osmans, because the activities in which they were engaged were not such as ought to give rise to one. There was no immunity because there was nothing for the police to be immune from.

These errors were shortly afterwards pointed out by Lord Browne-Wilkinson, delivering the leading judgment in the House of Lords in *Barrett v Enfield London Borough Council* (2001) 2 AC 550. This case was not about the liability of the police. It was about the corresponding rule that no duty of care was owed by local authorities engaged in child protection. The House felt bound by the decision in *Osman* to allow the action to go to trial, although they regarded it as legally misconceived. But they expressed the hope that the decision in *Osman* would be revisited. Lord Browne-Wilkinson observed (page 558) that the Strasbourg Court's decision in *Osman* was 'extremely difficult to understand'.

> Although the word 'immunity' is sometimes incorrectly used, a holding that it is not fair, just and reasonable to hold liable a particular class of defendants whether generally or in relation to a particular type of activity is not to give immunity from a liability to which the rest of the world is subject. It is a prerequisite to there being any liability in negligence at all that as a matter of policy it is fair, just and reasonable in those circumstances to impose liability in negligence.

The result of *Osman* was that for some years actions against the police and other public authorities could not be struck out. Instead, they were required to go through the ritual of a full trial only to fail later and at much greater cost for want of a relevant duty.

Osman was effectively overruled by the Grand Chamber of the Strasbourg Court in Z *and others v United Kingdom* (2002) 34 EHRR 3. This was another claim against a local authority for the negligent performance of its duty to protect children. It had been struck out as unarguable in the High Court, a decision ultimately affirmed by the House of Lords. By the time the case reached Strasbourg the explanation of Lord Browne-Wilkinson in *Barrett* was available. The subsequent course of events exposed the divisions within the Strasbourg Court. The Commission was entirely unrepentant. They invited the Court to stick to its analysis in *Osman*, on the ground that the claim must be regarded as arguable in English law, notwithstanding the decision of the House of Lords that it was not. This was, apparently, because the claimants had been granted legal aid and had won in the Court of Appeal. In reality, the Commission regarded the policy concerns that underlay the English law of tort as misguided. The majority of the Grand Chamber disagreed with the Commission. They accepted Lord Browne-Wilkinson's explanation of English law and held that it undermined the decision in *Osman*. They therefore rejected the complaint. However, in two joint judgments, four judges of the Grand Chamber dissented. Both judgments were essentially based on a dislike of the principles of the English law of negligence. Their authors held the view, which they took no trouble to conceal, that in a matter as important as the protection of children, there ought to have been a duty. One dissent appeared to deprecate as an 'immunity' any domestic law qualification of a general rule of liability if the qualification applied only to a specific category of persons or activities. It suggested that it had been inconsistent with Article 6 to strike out the claim on general policy grounds, even when the policy in question went to the very existence of a legal duty. The other dissent went further. It openly criticised what its authors called the refusal of the House of Lords to 'extend tortious liability for civil wrongs arising out of a duty of care by local authorities for child care'.

The decision of the Strasbourg Court in Z marked a schismatic moment in the development of Strasbourg's outlook. The outcome, however, was a notable vindication of the policy of constructive dialogue between the Court of Human Rights and the national courts. Yet in *Matthews v Minister of Defence* (2003) 1 AC 1163 (para. 140) Lord Walker observed that notwithstanding Z, the 'uncertain shadow of *Osman* still lies over this area of law'. This was because only six months after the decision in Z, the observations of the Strasbourg Court in *Fayed*, which had launched the Court on its campaign against so-called 'immunities', were repeated word for word in *Fogarty v United Kingdom* (2002) 34 EHRR 12 as if nothing had happened. This suggested that the repentance of the Court was limited to the question of duties of care, and that their basic analysis of immunities remained intact. I shall return to *Fogarty* in a moment.

The result of the *Osman* debacle was a certain amount of regrouping in two cases decided in 2005 and 2006. One was *Roche v United Kingdom* (2006) 42 EHRR 30. The other was *Markovic v Italy* (2007) 44 EHRR 52. *Roche* was about personal injuries suffered as a result of service in the armed forces. Under section 10 of the Crown Proceedings Act 1947 the Secretary of State was required to certify that the injuries had arisen from the claimant's service in the armed forces. The effect of the certificate was that the injured serviceman had no right to sue the Crown for negligence but enjoyed instead a right to a service disability pension without proof of fault. The Grand Chamber adopted a new approach. According to this approach, the application of Article 6 to immunities should depend on a distinction between the substantive and the procedural rules of domestic law. This of course was the very distinction that the Court had declined to draw in *Fayed*. But that case was disregarded as being, in this respect, a one-off decision on its facts. The Court distinguished between an immunity from liability and an immunity from suit. It held that an immunity from liability should be regarded as substantive and not subject to review under Article 6; whereas an immunity from suit should be regarded as procedural and open to review in accordance with the triple test of legitimacy, proportionality and consistency with the 'essence of the right'. In this case, the Court accepted the analysis of the House of Lords that a section 10 certificate was substantive, and concluded that therefore Article 6 had no application.

In *Markovic*, the applicants were a group of Yugoslav citizens seeking redress in the Italian courts for the death of their relatives in the NATO air raid on Belgrade in 1999, which had been launched from bases in Italy. These were said to be acts of war in violation of international law. The Corte di Cassazione had held that the Italian courts had no jurisdiction over acts of war or indeed over any acts of the Italian state which were impugned on the sole ground that they violated international law. The Strasbourg Court adopted the same distinction between substance and procedure as they had in *Roche*. They held that the limitation on the jurisdiction of the Italian court was substantive. The decision of the Corte di Cassazione, they said (para. 114), 'does not amount to recognition of an immunity but is merely indicative of the extent of the courts' powers of review of acts of foreign policy such as acts of war'.

The distinction between substance and procedure is certainly an improvement on the erratic approach previously adopted. But it is hardly satisfactory. It can be a very fine distinction indeed. Even when the distinction is clear, it is frequently arbitrary. And there are some rules of law that do not readily lend themselves to a simple classification as procedural or substantive.

Time bars are a good example. Limitation or prescription is an almost universal feature of developed systems of law. In England, limitation is a procedural defence. Except in the case of title to land, it bars the remedy but not the right. It follows that under current Strasbourg conceptions, its application to any particular case is subject to review for legitimacy and proportionality. This is what the Strasbourg Court held in *Stubbings v United Kingdom* (1997) 23 EHRR 213. In Scotland, limitation is also procedural, but prescription is substantive. It extinguishes the right. So it seems clear that if identical claims were barred by limitation in England

and prescription in Scotland, Article 6 would be engaged in England but not in Scotland. Indeed, this is what the Scottish courts have held: see *S v Miller (No 1)* 2001 SC 977. Plainly this is anomalous.

State immunity is a more controversial example. It is an almost universal rule of civilised nations, based on the equality of states in international law, who are not therefore entitled to sit in judgment on each other. The Strasbourg Court first grappled with state immunity in *Waite and Kennedy v Germany* (2000) 30 EHRR 261, a decision about the statutory immunity conferred by German law on the German operations of an intergovernmental organisation, the European Space Agency. The case was decided after *Osman* but before *Z*. The Court cited *Osman* as authority for the proposition that a rule of law which limits the application of some principle of liability to particular categories of persons must be treated as an immunity and subject to review for legitimacy and proportionality. But it went on to hold that the application of state immunity to a wrongful dismissal claim was justified. It reached the same conclusion in *Fogarty v United Kingdom* in 2002, a sex discrimination case brought against the United States by an employee of its London embassy. By the time that *Fogarty* was decided, the Court had retreated from *Osman*. But in its judgment, it repeated verbatim its earlier statement, simply deleting the reference to *Osman* and substituting a reference to the passage from *Waite and Kennedy* which had been based on *Osman*.

Once the Strasbourg Court began to adopt its distinction between substantive and procedural immunities, it had to put state immunity in one box or the other. In *Al-Adsani v United Kingdom* (2002) 34 EHRR 11, the Court decided that state immunity was procedural. It followed that a court giving effect to the immunity would have to justify it as legitimate and proportionate. This decision has been received with some perplexity by the English courts. What the Strasbourg Court seems to have meant by describing state immunity as procedural is that it does not go to the merits of the claim. It does not define the existence or extent of any legal duty. But it is certainly not procedural in any ordinary sense. State immunity is a rule of substantive law, the effect of which is that the Court has no jurisdiction. As Lord Bingham observed in *Jones v Saudi Arabia* (2007) I AC 270 (para. 14), Article 6 cannot confer on a court a jurisdiction which it does not have, and a state cannot be said to deny access to its court if it has no access to give. When *Jones v Saudi Arabia* reached Strasbourg, the Court was invited to reconsider *Al-Adsani*. But it simply reaffirmed the decision without so much as addressing the difficulties involved.

None of this mattered very much as long as the Court continued to hold that state immunity was justified. But there are signs that the Court has begun to carry its traditional hostility to special defences and jurisdictional voids rather further. In *Cudak v Lithuania* (2010) 51 EHRR 15 in 2010, the Grand Chamber held that Article 6 had been violated when the Lithuanian courts upheld a claim for state immunity in a case of unfair dismissal brought by a switchboard operator at the Polish embassy in Vilnius. The Strasbourg Court had nothing against the fairness or impartiality of the Lithuanian proceedings. They simply thought that the Lithuanian courts had got the answer wrong. They should not have regarded the employment of the applicant as an act of sovereign power, *jure imperii*. Precisely the same approach was adopted, with the same result, in *Sabeh El Leil v France* (2012) 54 EHRR 14 in 2011, another unfair dismissal case, this time brought by the head of the accounts department in the Kuwaiti embassy in Paris. The Strasbourg Court held that the Paris Court of Appeals had been wrong to find as a fact that the applicant's job had included participating in sovereign acts done in the course of the embassy's diplomatic business, and that it had thereby arrived at the wrong conclusion as a matter of French law. The Strasbourg Court may or may not have been right in the view that it took of the merits of these two cases. But it seems a surprising result of Article 6 that the European Court of Human Rights should act as a Court of Appeal from perfectly fair proceedings in national courts simply because it disagreed with the way in which those courts had applied their own law. It also opens up the prospect that the hitherto absolute immunity of states in respect of sovereign acts may have to be treated as a qualified immunity whose application must be assessed on a case-by-case basis depending on whether its application to particular facts can be regarded as proportionate. More recently, in *J. C. and others v Belgium* (2021) (unreported), the Court veered back towards the more traditional, and orthodox, view. It upheld a Belgian court decision dismissing on the ground of state immunity proceedings against the Holy See for failing to protect children from abuse by Catholic priests. The judgment appears to accept that it was not for the Court to go behind established rules of public international law. But it still purported to act like a Court of Appeal, treating Article 6 as authority to review the correctness of the Belgian court's reasoning.

Before the decision in *Roche*, the Strasbourg Court had subjected special defences to review under Article 6, whether they were procedural or substantive. It currently reviews them if they are procedural but not if they are substantive. But it is worth asking why they should be reviewable in either case. The effect of a bar on proceedings is exactly the same, namely that the claim will fail. A rule of law may be procedural and yet reflect fundamental legal policies of the forum governing the incidence of liability. If a national court entertains the claim but decides in perfectly fair and impartial proceedings that the bar applies, it is not easy to see how the litigant can be said to have been deprived of a court.

This problem was recently illustrated in dramatic terms by the controversial decision of the Grand Chamber in a case about climate change: *Verein KlimaSeniorinnen Schweiz v Switzerland* (9 April 2024). The main point at issue was whether Swiss law concerning climate change violated the applicants' right to private and family life under Article 8 of the Convention. The Court held that it did. This is not the place to go into that issue. But the Court also held that the applicants had been denied access to the Swiss courts. This was a surprising conclusion, for the applicants had been heard by the Swiss administrative tribunals, then on appeal to the Federal Appeal Court and finally in the Federal Supreme Court. No one suggested that the proceedings had been unfair. The applicants failed in all three courts because they were unable to show that they had any personal interest in the issue over and above that of the population at large. This was a question of jurisdiction, which was probably to be classified as procedural. But the principle applied represented an important public policy common to many jurisdictions. The courts will not receive an *actio popularis*, i.e. a public law action in which self-appointed guardians of the public interest seek to raise political complaints without any special interest of their own. The only reason why the Grand Chamber felt able to say that Article 6 was violated was that they disagreed with the way that the Swiss Courts had applied their own law. They thought that the Swiss courts had taken too optimistic a view of the likely timescale for a climate disaster and concluded that the applicants did have a sufficient interest. The exercise of what is essentially an appellate jurisdiction over the entirely fair proceedings of national courts is on the face of it an abuse of Article 6, which is concerned with access to a court and not with the correctness of its reasoning or its findings of fact.

My object in making these points is not to rubbish Article 6. Its express provisions are among the core principles of any civilised society. It has been a principle of English common law for at least three centuries. It has undoubtedly brought benefits both to the United Kingdom and to other member states of the Council of Europe, notably by objecting to practices that prevent court proceedings from being fairly conducted. To give just two examples in a UK context, it has forced the United Kingdom to reduce the anomalous role that the Home Secretary once had in criminal sentencing; and it has restricted attempts to allow the deployment of closed material in court proceedings without, I think, unduly impairing the interests of national security. Its potential impact on the somewhat brutal forensic practices of some former communist countries of eastern Europe seems likely to be even more beneficial. But these are questions that lie within the scope of the core values of Article 6. The problem really lies with the appetite that the Strasbourg Court has demonstrated over the past half-century to transform the Convention into what in *Loizidou v Turkey* (1998) 26 EHRR CD5 it called an 'instrument of the European public order'. This has resulted in the application of Article 6 in areas well beyond its core values, in a way that appears to have little to do with the fairness of proceedings or even access to a court.

In his dissent in *Golder*, Sir Gerald Fitzmaurice warned that the implication into the Convention of rights which were not expressed there would lead to the development of a class of human rights with no exact definition and no principled limits. That prophecy has been borne out by events. Opinions will differ about whether these additional rights are desirable. Like, I suspect, most lawyers, I think that the picture is mixed. Some are desirable while others are not. What seems clear, however, is that the result has been to expose the European Court of Human Rights to accusations of altering principles of civil liability in ways that are practically incapable of amendment or repeal by national legislatures. It is open to doubt whether Article 6 was ever intended to serve such a far-reaching purpose. But that is unlikely to worry a court that has resolved to emancipate itself from the intentions of the states party to the Convention.

XI

THE EUROPEAN UNION AND
THE NATION STATE*

What happens when an irresistible force collides with an immovable object? We are told by materials scientists that there are no such things as irresistible forces or immovable objects. But, philosophically and legally, there are. It is possible for an issue to arise on two fundamental and mutually inconsistent premises. In this chapter, I want to consider one notable example. The irresistible force is the primacy of European law in the legal orders of member states of the European Union. The immovable object is the body of domestic constitutional law which determines the limits on what a member state can do. In recent years a number of national courts have declined to apply EU law to questions arising under their national constitutions, thus provoking a direct conflict between them and the Court of Justice of the European Union. These cases raise some of the most profound questions that any political community can ask about itself. What is the basic building block of the international order? What is the ultimate source of political and legal authority in the societies in which we live? What are the defining characteristics of the state and does the European

---

* This was originally delivered as the John Kelly Memorial Lecture at University College Dublin, Sutherland School of Law, in March 2022.

Union possess those characteristics? If we have multiple identities, as most of us do, we have to ask which is the dominant one when they point in different directions. These questions have implications extending far beyond the European Union. The conundrum is of interest even in the United Kingdom, which is no longer an EU member.

In October 2021 Poland's Constitutional Court ruled that its constitution prevailed over European law. The background was the dispute over the independence of the Polish judiciary, which had been rumbling on ever since the Law and Justice Party won power in the Polish elections of 2015. The European Commission instituted proceedings against Poland, on the principal ground that changes made by the Law and Justice Party to the appointment and retirement of judges undermined the independence of the judiciary and discriminated against women. In 2019, the European Court upheld the Commission's complaint. The Polish Constitutional Court, now composed entirely of nominees of the Law and Justice Party, held that the European Court of Justice had exceeded its competence under the EU Treaty by purporting to rule on the constitutionality of judicial appointments. This, it held, was exclusively a matter for Poland and depended on its internal constitutional order.

Similar issues have arisen in other EU states. There has been a broader dispute between the EU and Hungary, which arises from the efforts of Mr Viktor Orbán's government to transform Hungary into a one-party state. His technique has been to use his large parliamentary majority to ensure that all the levers of influence and power are pulled by the Fidesz Party. More recently, the temperature has risen as a result of the decision of the European Court on 16 February 2022, authorising the Commission to withhold convergence funds from Poland and Hungary, without going through the procedures in Article 7 for suspending members' rights, which would require a unanimous decision of the other member states.

On 21 December 2021, the Court of Justice of the European Union handed down a judgment on a reference from the High Court of Romania. The High Court had convicted a number of prominent Romanian politicians of corruption. The Constitutional Court of Romania had quashed the conviction on the grounds that the High Court had been improperly constituted. Panels in the High Court are selected for assignment to particular cases by lot, but it appears that one of the five judges sitting on the case had not been selected in that way. The Court of Justice ruled that the decision of the Constitutional Court had been contrary to the rule of law, first, because it undermined attempts to suppress corruption in Romania, some of which affected EU funds; second, because the failure to constitute the panel by lot did not affect the judicial character of the conviction; and, third, because the decision infringed the principle of judicial independence.* The response of the Constitutional Court followed just two days later on 23 December 2021. It took the form of a press release of uncertain legal status, criticising the reasoning of the Luxembourg court and declaring that it would not be lawful in Romania to comply with it without a constitutional amendment.†

I am not proposing to address the legal or political merits of what these three states have done. My concern is with the wider juridical implications of the conflict, in particular the relationship between EU law and national constitutions. The issue can be stated in this way. When a state becomes a member of the European Union, it transfers part of its legislative and judicial sovereignty to the European Union.

---

*Joined Cases C-357/19, C-379/19, C-547/19, C-811/19, C-840/19.
† www.ccr.ro/en/press-release-23-december-2021.

On the face of it, this means that the powers of the EU's institutions depend on the extent of the transfer. As a matter of international law, the transfer is effected by the EU treaties, of which the European Court of Justice is the ultimate interpreter. But as a matter of the domestic law of member states, the transfer is effected under national law. This may happen either because the constitution of a signatory state gives automatic and overriding effect to treaties as part of its domestic law, or else because ordinary legislation is enacted to give effect to it. The former is the approach adopted by monist states, the latter by dualist states. But in either case, the reception of treaty law into the domestic legal order of a member state depends on its domestic law, whose interpretation is exclusively a matter for national courts. So what if EU law as interpreted by the European Court of Justice and national law as interpreted by its highest domestic constitutional court arrive at inconsistent conclusions?

The two founding doctrines of the European Union are the 'principle of conferral', that European institutions enjoy only the competences conferred on them by member states by treaty; and the primacy of European law in the legal order of its member states. Neither of these principles was expressly set out in the original treaties which created the European Economic Community. But they were implicit from the outset, and have been endorsed in successive judgments of the European Court of Justice. They are an essential part of the constitutional architecture of the European Union. This is because in the absence of a common European identity, the European Union is no more or less than a body of common rules. Without them, there is no Union. The European Commission can afford to lose on the question of whether Poland and Hungary have departed from the fundamental values of the EU. It cannot afford to lose on the question which law prevails.

The answer given by the European Court of Justice has been consistent throughout. European law prevails. Always. This was first stated in two famous cases decided in the 1960s: *Van Gend en Loos* in 1963* and *Costa v ENEL* in 1964.† *Van Gend en Loos* is the leading authority for the doctrine of direct effect. The Dutch government contended that the EC treaties, like any other treaties, were binding in international law as between the EEC and each member state, but had no direct impact on the rights and obligations of citizens as a matter of domestic law. In rejecting this contention, the Luxembourg Court acknowledged that that would ordinarily be the effect of a multilateral treaty between states. But they made the radical claim that the founding treaty of the EEC was 'more than an agreement which merely creates mutual obligations between the contracting states'. It created a new legal order that superseded the legislative autonomy of member states in the areas within the competence of the EEC. *Costa v ENEL*, which followed a year later, was an even more radical assertion of the existence of a new legal order. The treaty constituting the European Economic Community was incorporated into Italian law by a specially enacted Italian statute of 1957. The issue was whether an Italian law of 1962 nationalising the electricity industry was compatible with it. In a parallel case, the Italian Constitutional Court had held that the extent to which the EEC treaties were received into Italian domestic law was, on the face of it, a question of Italian law for the Italian courts. The Italian statute of 1957 that had received European law into its domestic legal order could be repealed or amended by subsequent legislation like any other statute. Therefore, if the statutory nationalisation of the electricity industry was incompatible with EU law, the

---

* Case 26/62.
† Case 6/64.

incorporation of EU law into the domestic law of Italy must to that extent be regarded as amended. The response of the European Court of Justice was that the treaty represented a higher order of law, displacing Italian legislative sovereignty.

These decisions laid down three principles. First, it is for EU law to decide which system of law should answer the question of primacy. Second, that question must itself be answered solely by reference to EU law. Third, by EU law, EU law is to prevail. In substance, they were saying that the treaty was not simply decisive on the plane of international law. It was itself a constitutional act by which in areas within the EU's competence a member state's legal and political identity is subsumed in a larger entity. In its judgment in the Romanian case that I have just cited, the Court of Justice restated these principles. In sum, they said, the treaties constituting the European Union, were what they called 'a constitutional charter' for the community and each of its members. In effect, there was a European constitution which prevailed over the national constitutions of member states, as if the latter were simply regional sub-constitutions.

The problems posed by this analysis can best be illustrated by a glance at the best-known historical example of a union superseding in limited areas the autonomy of its component parts – the United States of America. The Constitution of the United States declares itself to be the 'supreme law of the land'. By acceding to it, the component states agree that the Constitution is to supersede their own constitutions and their own substantive laws so far as they conflict. But there are significant differences between the United States and the European Union. In the first place, the European Union is not a state, but an international organisation of states whose members pool their sovereignty in certain areas. Secondly, the states of the USA had a far higher degree of cultural and political homogeneity in the late eighteenth century than the nations of Europe had in the twentieth. Thirdly, the United States is not dependant on the states for the application of federal law. It controls the reserve of force which is the ultimate basis of all political and legislative authority. The President is the Supreme Commander not just of the armed forces of the Union but also of the state militias when they are called upon. This is perhaps the most striking example of a new legal order displacing in defined areas the sovereignty of its constituent parts. The issue was dramatically tested in the Civil War, when the Union declined to recognise the Confederate states' right to secede and imposed on them laws passed by Congress during the period when the southern representatives had withdrawn from it. This was a forthright assertion of the principle that the US Constitution had created a new political identity for its component states. By comparison, the European Union has expressly accepted the right of member states to secede since the Lisbon treaty, and implicitly did so even before that.

There are some legal issues that cannot be resolved by legal analysis, because they depend on what jurists have sometimes called 'fundamental constitutional facts'. If the EU asserts the primacy of its own law and the member states assert the primacy of their own constitutions, and neither of them backs down, the conflict can only be resolved by a trial of political strength. In other words, the outcome must depend on fundamental constitutional facts. The idea that EU law derives its force from a new pan-European constitutional order, displacing the legal order of member states in areas within its competence, can only work if either the constitutional organs of the member states accept it as a matter of their domestic law, or else the organs of the European Union are able to impose it not just by law but by force.

This issue has emerged with special intensity in the countries of eastern Europe, but it is not peculiar to them.

The leading judicial champion of the primacy of national constitutions over European law is not Poland, Hungary or Romania. It is Germany. I want to focus on the decisions of the German constitutional court, the *Bundesverfassungsgericht*. They are important partly because of the political and juridical weight of Germany in the European Union and partly because of the high quality and detailed reasoning of its judgments. In a series of decisions, the German Constitutional Court has subjected the domestic application of European law to certain constitutional conditions under German domestic law. These are sometimes called the '*so lange*' decisions. *So lange wie* is the expression of conditionality in German. It means 'provided that'.

Germany has incorporated European law into its domestic legal order by its constitution, but only in qualified terms. Article 25 of the Basic Law (the *Grundgesetz*) provides that international law is an integral part of domestic law and prevails over domestic statutes. Articles 23 and 24 empower the German legislature to transfer sovereign powers to a European Union that is committed to 1) the rule of law, 2) the principle of subsidiarity, and 3) the protection of basic rights equivalent to those conferred by the Basic Law itself. These three things have been interpreted as conditions for the application of European law to Germany. In addition, the Constitutional Court has recognised a number of implied conditions, arising from the character and identity of the German state as the foundation of German civil society.

In 1974, in *Internationale Handelsgesellschaft*, usually called *Solange I*,* the Constitutional Court accepted in principle the primacy of European law. But it held that without a constitutional amendment international obligations could not prevail over what it called 'the fundamental principles of the

---

*2 BvR 52/71.

Constitution, forming the basis of its identity'. It followed, they said, that European law could not prevail over funda- mental rights conferred by the German constitution which had no substantial equivalent in the law of the European Union. Twelve years later, in 1986, the Court retreated from that position in *Wunsche Handelsgesellschaft*, sometimes called *Solange II*.* It held that the recognition of human rights by the institutions of the EU and the creation of a directly elected parliament had reduced the scope for conflict. So, while the Court retained its power to review European legislation for conformity with the constitution, it would in future refrain from exercising that power.

As a result, the issue largely disappeared until it re-emerged when the competences of European institutions were enlarged in the 1990s and later. The main milestones were monetary union following the treaty of Maastricht and the enhancement of the legislative role of the European Par- liament in the Lisbon treaty. In 1993, in *Brunner*, the Court heard a constitutional challenge to the Maastricht treaty, and in particular to the transfer of monetary policy to the insti- tutions of the European Union. The challenge failed. But the Court developed a new principle under which it was entitled to review the powers conferred on Europe by the treaties and in appropriate cases declare the exercise of those powers by European institutions to be *ultra vires* and ineffective in Germany. This was held to be a question of domestic law, because it was under that law that the powers had been con- ferred on the European Union. European law, they declared 'can only have binding effects within the German sovereign sphere by virtue of the German instruction that its law be applied'.[†]

---

*2 BvR 197/83.
†2 BvR 2134/92, 2159/92.

Subsequently, the tone was been set by a remarkable judgment of the Constitutional Court on the Lisbon treaty in 2009.* The decision arose out of a constitutional challenge to the right of the German state to ratify the treaty, on the ground that it restricted the legislative autonomy of Germany. Once again, the challenge failed. But in rejecting it, the Court developed a wide-ranging concept of constitutional identity. It held that Germany could not transfer legislative powers that undermined either the constitutional identity of the German state or its ultimate right of self-determination. This meant that it could not recognise any claim of the European Union's institutions to determine the extent of their own legal powers. They must always be subject to the limits of the powers conferred on Europe by national law. Those limits had to be determined as a matter of national law by national courts. The most interesting part of the Court's analysis was the section in which it identified those things that were fundamental to a country's existence as a sovereign state and were not amenable to transfer to a supranational body. They were the areas of policy that, in the Court's words, depended on 'cultural historical and linguistic perceptions'. They included citizenship; control of the organs of force, i.e. the police and the armed forces; control of public revenue and expenditure; criminal law; education, family life, faith and collective ideology; and, more generally, those matters that shape the living conditions of citizens. The Court pointed out that in spite of the growing integration of Europe, the public's political perceptions were still largely moulded by the nation state and its language, history and culture. In other words, democracy remained essentially national and not, or not yet, European. No other judicial decision in any country has explored the question of national

---

* 2 BvE 2/08.

identity in such depth. I suggested earlier that the conflict between European law and national constitutions could only be resolved by a trial of political strength, by some ultimate constitutional fact. This decision sets out the ultimate constitutional facts as clearly as any that I know.

One of the factors listed in the Lisbon treaty judgment as making up the German identity was the control of public revenue and expenditure. I doubt whether many countries would have included that item, but its inclusion reflected one of the most powerful political instincts in modern German history, the fear of uncontrolled inflation of the kind that nearly ruined Germany in the 1920s, contributing to the political instability of the following years and the rise of Nazism. This was the unspoken fact that lay behind the series of decisions from 2012 onward in which the *Bundesverfassungsgericht* laid down limits on Germany's right to participate in the European Stability Mechanism and then in the European Central Bank's programme of purchases of member states' public debt. The complaint against them was that they could potentially involve Germany in assuming obligations fixed by the European Central Bank or by the majority of participating states, and not by German constitutional procedures. The most recent and controversial of these judgments was given in May 2020 in *Weiss*.* *Weiss* was a complex case that is not easy to analyse. The European Central Bank had exclusive competence in the area of monetary policy in the eurozone, but not in the area of economic policy. In 2015 it embarked upon a programme of purchases of Greek public debt, with a view to spreading the risk of a Greek default across the national central banks of the eurozone including, of course, the Bundesbank. Mr Weiss was one of four Eurosceptic politicians who complained in the

---

*2 BvR 859/15, 1651/15, 2006/15, 980/16.

Constitutional Court that the Bundesbank and the federal government should have opposed the programme, because it meant that a Greek default might require the Bundesbank to be recapitalised at the expense of the German taxpayer. His main argument was that, viewed as purely monetary measures, the purchases were disproportionate because the monetary benefits were not worth the risk. But, he complained, they were not really monetary measures. They were a disguised exercise of powers of economic management that the European Central Bank did not possess. The *Bundesverfassungsgericht* referred this question, among others, to the European Court in Luxembourg. Luxembourg answered that the measures were properly to be classified as monetary measures and were proportionate. When the case returned to the *Bundesverfassungsgericht*, it rejected that answer. It began by reiterating that financial autonomy and exclusive control of public revenue and expenditure were fundamental to Germany's constitutional identity. It then went on to hold that the European Central Bank's proportionality analysis was defective because it did not take account of all the economic consequences of the debt purchases. The European Court of Justice's endorsement of the European Central Bank's proportionality analysis was said to be 'incomprehensible' and therefore beyond the competence of the European Court. Unless and until the Central Bank did another proportionality analysis on the principles favoured by the *Bundesverfassungsgericht*, it could not conclude that the Bank had acted within its competence either. Its decision could therefore have no legal effect in Germany.

Weiss is a most extreme decision. This is because the Court's basic criticism of the Court of Justice was that it got the proportionality test wrong. But even if it did, the error did not on the face of it go to jurisdiction. The Court of Justice was undoubtedly competent to decide the issue. Its judgment was not *ultra vires* simply because it got the answer wrong in the view of a national court. The logic of the German court's position is that every national court would be entitled to decline to receive European law as declared by the Luxembourg court on the ground that it disagreed. The legislation of the European Union would then have to comply with the analytical methods of every one of its twenty-seven national systems as a condition of its recognition in their domestic legal order. Interestingly, the European Commission brought infringement proceedings against Germany. Constitutionally, the function of defending Germany fell to its government. The German government, however, declined to defend the decision. The Commission closed its proceedings in December 2021 on the grounds that it had received suitable assurances from Germany. But those assurances had come from the government. Since the Constitutional Court is independent of the government, the very principle that the Commission has invoked against Poland, the acceptance of German government assurances looks very much like a political fudge. The Commission does not want to take on Germany but would prefer to concentrate its fire on weaker countries like Poland that are more dependent on EU funds.

The principle that there are inalienable powers fundamental to a state's constitutional identity that cannot be undermined by EU law without a sufficiently national constitutional amendment, has been developed further by the German court than by any other. But it is in fact common to almost every national legal system that has considered the question. The consensus of European domestic jurisprudence has been that European law prevails over ordinary domestic law but not over national constitutions. Ironically, one of the most robust statements came from the Polish Constitutional Court at a time well before any question arose as to its independence. In its decision of May 2005 on Poland's

accession to the European Union, the Court declared that
the Polish constitution was 'the supreme act expressing the
nation's will'. European law could not therefore prevail over
a constitutional norm or limit its application. Any conflict
would have to be resolved either by a constitutional amendment or by leaving the European Union.* This is exactly
the same principle as the *Bundesverfassungsgericht* declared
four years later in its review of the treaty of Lisbon. In Italy,
the Constitutional Court reserved to itself as early as 1974
the right to question the application of EU law when it
potentially infringed what it called 'supreme constitutional
principles' of the Italian state. In the case of *Frontini*, it established that EU law did not prevail over the fundamental
principles of the Italian constitution or the inalienable rights
of citizens. This was because Article XI of the Italian constitution, which authorised limitations of sovereignty in the
interests of world peace, was confined to measures directed
to that end.† France is a monist jurisdiction whose constitution directly incorporates its international obligations into
domestic law. Nonetheless, the Constitutional Council has
ruled, borrowing the language of the *Bundesverfassungsgericht*, that an EU Directive could not require the state to
legislate contrary to the 'constitutional identity of France'.‡
When the Constitutional Council came to review the Lisbon
treaty, it approved its ratification on the ground that the constitution made specific provision for the incorporation of
treaties into the domestic legal order. But it warned that a
constitutional amendment would be required before France
could recognise domestically a European measure that

---

*Trybunal Konstytucyjni K18/04.
† Corte Costtituzionale 183/1973.
‡ 2006/540 DC, 27 juillet 2006, para. 19); 2011-631 DC, 9 juin 2011,
para. 45.

'called into question constitutionally guaranteed rights and freedoms or adversely affected the fundamental conditions on which national sovereignty is exercised.'* The Constitutional Court of Spain has held, in reviewing the treaty of Nice, that general provisions of the constitution authorising the application of European law domestically may not undermine the sovereignty of the state, its basic constitutional structures or the fundamental principles and values of the constitution.† In its own leading case, *Crotty v An Taoiseach*, the Supreme Court of Ireland held in its review of the Single European Act that the transfer of any substantial aspect of the legislative or governmental sovereignty of the state would be unconstitutional if enacted by ordinary legislation. It would require a constitutional amendment.‡ Similar declarations can be found in the constitutional jurisprudence of the Czech Republic, Denmark, Estonia and Latvia.§

It is perhaps surprising to find the United Kingdom in this distinguished company. The United Kingdom is the only European country that has no written constitution and therefore no body of fundamental law with which European law can be said to be inconsistent. When Britain first agreed to join what was then the European Economic Community, Mr Blackburn, a prominent Eurosceptic, applied to the High Court for a declaration that the government had no power to surrender essential features of Britain's sovereignty to an international body. The court accepted that this would be the consequence of joining the EEC, citing *Costa v ENEL*. But Mr Blackburn's claim was struck out as unarguable.¶

---

*2007/560 DC, 20 December 2007, para. 9.
†DTC 1/2004.
‡[1987] I.R. 713.
§US 50/04 (Czech Republic), Højesteret I 361/1997 (Denmark), Riigikohus 3-4-1-6-12 (Estonia), Satversmestiesa 2008-35-01 (Latvia).
¶*Blackburn v Attorney General* (1987) 1 W.L.R. 1037.

Yet his basic argument was the same as the argument that has now been accepted in principle by most of the constitutional courts of Europe. They have implicitly rejected the more ambitious claims of the Luxembourg court in *Costa v ENEL*. The difference is that whereas the British Parliament has unlimited political and legislative sovereignty, every other European state operates under formal constitutions that limit the power of the legislature in the absence of a constitutional amendment. The European Communities Act 1972 provided the statutory basis for Britain's membership of the European Union. Nonetheless, in the course of Britain's forty-seven-year membership its courts were eventually forced to recognise some limitations on the primacy of European law. They began to recognise a class of 'constitutional statutes', which could not be repealed or amended by implication whenever a later statute was inconsistent with it. They could be repealed or amended only explicitly. One of these was the European Communities Act 1972. The result, at a Divisional Court held in *Thoburn v Sunderland City Council* in 1987, was that European law applied in the United Kingdom only so far as that Act allowed. Lord Justice Laws, delivering the judgment of the Court, pointed out that the application of EU law in the United Kingdom depended on its domestic law and not on EU law. It followed, as he went on to observe, that 'in the event, which no doubt would never happen in the real world, that a European measure was seen to be repugnant to a fundamental or constitutional right guaranteed by the law of England, a question would arise whether the general words of the 1972 Act were sufficient to incorporate the measure and give it overriding effect in domestic law'.*

In fact, it nearly did happen in the real world. The environmental legislation of the European Union contains

---

*[2003] Q.B. 151, at [69].

provisions that empower national legislatures to authorise environmentally sensitive projects, but only after proper scrutiny. This is uncontroversial in countries where constitutional courts can review the acts of the legislature. But in the British constitutional tradition it is anathema. Article 9 of the Bill of Rights 1689, perhaps the ultimate constitutional statute, provides that proceedings in Parliament are not to be questioned in any court of law. In *HS2 Alliance Ltd v Secretary of State for Transport* the Supreme Court found it possible to decide the case without reference to this issue, but it observed that 'if there is a conflict between a constitutional principle, such as that embodied in article 9 of the Bill of Rights, and EU law, that conflict has to be resolved by our courts as an issue arising under the constitutional law of the United Kingdom'. The relevant UK law was the European Communities Act 1972. The Court thought that that Act would not be clear enough to authorise a violation of a fundamental feature of British constitutional law.* What the Supreme Court was doing was the same as the *Bundesverfassungsgericht* had been doing since 1974: it was implying into British constitutional statutes limitations to protect the fundamentals of the constitution. In *Miller v Secretary of State for Exiting the European Union* in 2016 the Supreme Court returned to this theme, observing that 'legislation which alters the domestic constitutional status of EU institutions or of EU law is not constrained by the need to be consistent with EU law. In the case of such legislation, there is no question of EU law having primacy, so that such legislation will have domestic effect even if it infringes EU law.'†

The conflict between EU law and national constitutions is one of the places where law and politics meet. It can be

---

*[2014] UKSC 3, at [78]–[79].
†[2017] UKSC 5 at [67].

resolved by some ultimate constitutional fact, in effect a trial of political strength. I am dealing now with law, not politics. So I do not want to delve too far into the domestic politics of the United Kingdom. There is, however, an obvious connection between the idea of constitutional identity, which underlies the jurisprudence of so many national constitutional courts of Europe, and the sentiments that persuaded a narrow majority of the British electorate to vote to leave the European Union in the referendum of 2016. Personally, I regret that decision. I think that it was a serious mistake. But I have always tried to warn against the facile view that the vote was due to xenophobia, post-imperial nostalgia, lies written on the side of campaign buses or other such nonsense explanations. The British knew what they were doing. They did it out of a sense of national constitutional identity, and a fear of seeing that identity subordinated to a larger and more distant European polity. These feelings were not as carefully articulated as the judgments of the German and other constitutional courts. But they were equally powerful. As the German court has pointed out, there is as yet no European identity to supersede the national identities of member states, nothing to which the mass of European citizens can feel a common and overriding loyalty. Until there is one, the tensions that I have been discussing will persist. In any democracy, real conflicts that cannot be resolved legally will sooner or later have to be resolved politically.

FREEDOM OF SPEECH

XII

THE NEW ROUNDHEADS: POLITICS
AND THE MISUSE OF HISTORY*

Over the past two decades, a number of intolerant ideologies have swept through the worlds of learning, literature and the visual and performing arts. It is a large subject, but I propose to address just one of these ideologies. Its essential feature is the diversion of academic disciplines to a task for which they are usually ill-suited, namely the reform of modern society so as to redress perceived inequalities, notably of race. In the course of this exercise, some of these disciplines have been discredited and others distorted, generally with little or no factual basis. The study of history is particularly vulnerable to this process. Most historical scholarship involves judicious selection from a vast and usually incomplete body of material. It is possible, by tendentious selection, to create an entirely false narrative without actually lying. The major threat to historical integrity arises when the criteria of selection are derived from a modern ideological agenda. What we have been witnessing is the reshaping of the history of the last four centuries to serve as a weapon in current political disputes. Objectivity and truth have been the main casualties of this process.

---

* This a lightly edited version of a Pharos Lecture, delivered at the Sheldonian Theatre in Oxford in February 2023.

I shall start with a well-known example which perfectly illustrates the problem. In November 2022, the Wellcome Collection, a museum dedicated to the history of medicine, announced the closure of Medicine Man, an exhibition of artefacts relating to the history of medicine collected by its founder Sir Henry Wellcome. The decision to close this exhibition was itself perfectly reasonable. As a collector, Sir Henry Wellcome was a bit of a magpie, and the exhibition, which was fifteen years old, was rather fusty. However, what mainly attracted attention was the statement that the curators published on Twitter. They said that they had closed it because it 'perpetuates a version of medical history that is based on racist, sexist and ableist theories and language'. To understand this statement, it is necessary to go back two and a half years to an earlier announcement from the Wellcome Collection in June 2020 in the aftermath of the murder of George Floyd in Minneapolis. Under the heading 'Anti-Blackness and Racism', it declared that the Collection was built on 'racist and patriarchal narratives' and that institutional racism was enmeshed within its fabric. It went on to suggest that not only the Wellcome Collection but museums generally were 'built on a foundation of white supremacy' and had replicated 'racist behaviours' for decades. The curators declared their intention of 'continually ask[ing] questions about power, representation and the civic role of public museums' and focusing on the 'lived experiences of those who have been silenced, erased and ignored'.

What does all that mean? It is palpably untrue that medical history, as presented in Medicine Man, was based on racist, sexist and ableist theories. Certainly, museums reflect the historical outlook of those who assembled their collections and their successors who curated them. In Britain, they were generally able-bodied white males. But museums do not, just by virtue of that fact, replicate racist behaviours.

Nor does our culture silence or ignore non-European experience where it is relevant. What, I think, the curators meant to say was that the exhibition treated medicine as a Western science of which non-white groups were passive consumers with no worthwhile contribution of their own. This, they felt, implied a hierarchy of cultures in which the West was superior to the rest, a notion that was offensive to non-Western racial groups.

The Wellcome Collection is not alone. The Museum Association, which represents museums generally, has called on them to 'address colonial structures and approaches to all areas of museum work'. At about the same time as the curators of the Wellcome Collection published their June 2020 statement, the Director of the Royal Botanical Gardens at Kew, probably the world's leading institution dedicated to plant science, issued a similar statement on its behalf. He began with the usual cringing confession that its history 'shamefully draws from a legacy that has deep roots in colonialism and racism'. The only fact cited to support this surprising assertion is that during the nineteenth century, the Royal Botanical Gardens studied the movement of plants around the British Empire as part of its worldwide botanical mission. This is said to have made the Botanical Gardens at Kew a 'beacon of privilege and exploitation'. The director went on to declare that Kew would in future decolonise its collections and 'tackle structural racism in plant and fungal science', with a view to achieving 'transformative societal change' in modern Britain. The inference is that merely by having existed and collected information and specimens in the great age of imperialism, Kew Gardens is in some way complicit in modern inequalities in Britain. Finally this: 'There is no acceptable neutral position on this subject [racial injustice]; to stay silent is to be complicit.' This is a particularly odd thing to say. It seems obvious that one can be an excellent plant scientist and an outstanding plant historian without taking any view at all on racial injustice.

These statements, and there are many others of the same kind, have certain points in common.

The first is that they are proposing a political programme for the modern day, supported by a highly selective approach to the past that sees everything through the prism of race. Race becomes the supremely important phenomenon, masking every other aspect of a complex culture. Racial politics provide the framework of values by which every institution concerned with the past is to be judged. This is a curiously slanted point of view. There are many important factors in the way that human societies develop. Race is only one of them and not necessarily the most important. Any serious commentator on the current state of historical studies ought to welcome attempts to present aspects of history that have previously been ignored or marginalised. That includes the story of ethnic minorities and non-European societies. But it does not mean that the whole of Britain's modern history should be viewed through their eyes. It does not mean that the role of slavery or empire in Britain's economic, cultural and social history should be exaggerated beyond recognition. And it does not mean that current political priorities should determine how we understand the past.

The second thing that these statements by various museums have in common is that they lose sight of the broader evolution of human history. Benjamin Disraeli once observed in response to an antisemitic taunt in the House of Commons, that 'while the ancestors of the right honourable gentleman were brutal savages in an unknown island, mine were priests in the temple of Solomon'. Victorian elites undoubtedly regarded their own civilisation as superior to others. This been a universal habit of humanity ever since the Greek city-states and the ancient dynasties of China

dismissed the rest of the world as barbarians. If these prejudices are ever justified, it is only for short periods of time,
two or three centuries at the most. Empires and cultures are
transient. They have their periods of power and creativity
before fading away. Medicine is as good an example as any.
White males have not always dominated medical science.
There have been periods when the major contributions came
from non-European cultures – Chinese, Indian and Arab in
particular. Historians have not ignored this. Great books have
been written about it, almost all of them in European lan-
guages. The twenty-six volumes of the *History of Science and
Technology in China* by the Cambridge scientist and historian
Joseph Needham is one of the most remarkable works ever
written on the multicultural origins of modern science. But
this should not blind us to the fact that the three centuries
before the Second World War were European centuries, in
medicine as in other sciences. With very few exceptions, such
as the use of some medicinal plants, indigenous non-Euro-
peans contributed very little. If one looks across a broader
chronological range, the picture is very different. But calls
for the decolonisation of academic disciplines do not do
that. They generally focus narrowly on the eighteenth and
nineteenth centuries and seek to debunk one of the few indis-
putable facts about that period, namely that it was a period
in which cultural and scientific developments fundamental
to the modern world almost all emanated from Europe or
from European settlements elsewhere.

Museums have been among the most visible and vocal
exponents of the current calls for decolonisation. But it
has affected every intellectual discipline concerned with
the past and many that are not. In Oxford, the Faculty of
Classics is one of many that have made public statements
about the legacy of colonialism. Its website declares that
the origins of the Oxford Classics degree are 'embedded

in a nineteenth-century colonial context'. This is said to be because of what the document calls 'civilisational thinking', in other words the view that there is a hierarchy of cultures with the West at the top. The document goes on to point out that when Classics became a distinct school at Oxford at the beginning of the nineteenth century, British elites viewed the classical world as a superior civilisation and adopted Classics as a guarantee of the standing of their own civilisation. All this is true, but it had nothing to do with colonialism or empire. It originated in humanist educational ideals of the sixteenth century that were common to all of Europe including countries with no colonial tradition. The same educational ideals were prominent, for example, in Germany, whose universities were major centres of classical philology, archaeology and history long before Germany developed colonial aspirations of its own.

Decolonisation has been demanded of many other disciplines that were never in any meaningful sense colonised: the visual arts, music, literature, philosophy, and even the physical sciences and mathematics. The only connection between these fields of study and Europe's imperial past is that the West achieved a dominant position in them during the imperial era. One does not have to go far to encounter some remarkable examples. The decolonisation statement of Oxford's Mathematical, Physical and Life Sciences Division reveals the same obsession with race and the same tendentious attempt to portray racism as a perennial theme of Western thinking. It begins by seeking to discredit its own subject by referring to the scientific racism of the nineteenth century, which posited a racial hierarchy identified by physiological characteristics, a view that no serious scientist has entertained for many decades and that has no current relevance to the subject. It goes on to identify science with empire by pointing to the Victorians' collection of material samples and botanical specimens across the globe. Moving to the present day, it calls for a study of deep-rooted racial biases in digital technology, artificial intelligence and machine learning. One would have thought that these subjects were incapable of racial bias, with the arguable exception of artificial intelligence, which may not be ideologically neutral. But as the statement proceeds, it becomes clear that the real object of the statement is to redefine knowledge itself in a way that devalues Western science. 'As we work towards greater inclusion', it declares, 'we need to have a broader understanding of what constitutes "scientific knowledge"'. Among other things, this is said to involve 'challenging western-centric ideas of "objectivity", "expertise" and "merit"', and 'removing structural hierarchies that privilege certain knowledge and certain peoples over others'. It is clear that the authors of this document believe that empirical scientific methods as they have been conceived in the West since the seventeenth century are just one of a number of equally valid approaches to the subject, and that it racially biased to prefer it to any other.

There are two basic ideas behind statements like these. One is about the nature of historical truth. The other is about inherited collective guilt.

The repeated emphasis on challenging the structures of power, which one sees in the statements of the Wellcome Collection and the Mathematical, Physical and Life Sciences Division of Oxford University, is an echo of the teaching of postmodernist philosophers like Michel Foucault. Foucault was the leading exponent of the idea that objective truth is unattainable, because truth is by nature subjective. In *The Archaeology of Knowledge* (published in 1969), he taught that the structures of power within a society determine what is generally perceived to be true. Few people outside the discipline of philosophy have read Foucault's opaque works. But many more have read Edward Said's influential book *Orientalism*, published in 1978, which applied Foucault's ideas to the legacy of the great European empires. Said argued that powerful groups control the intellectual framework within which ideas are discussed, and determine what constitutes knowledge. Historical truth, he claimed, is not discovered. It is made by historians, in accordance with unconscious prejudices moulded by the power structures of society. The power structures that had enabled Europeans to dominate much of the world between the eighteenth and the twentieth centuries had generated a view of the world based on a hierarchy of civilisations that patronised and marginalised non-European peoples. According to Said, this frame of mind persisted. It led modern scholars to construct a narrative of the past that treated non-Western races as representing an earlier stage of human evolution, less valid than the more developed experience of the modern West. The task of the historian was therefore to deconstruct the hegemonic West and substitute a different power structure in which other people's truth could be acknowledged.

These ideas have been extremely influential among many people who know nothing of their origin and have never heard of Foucault or Said. In 2015 the organisers of the campaign to remove the statue of Cecil Rhodes from its niche outside Oriel College issued a pamphlet entitled *Our Aims*. Their purpose, it said, was to suppress the frame of mind that the statue symbolised. It was to 'remedy the highly selective narrative of traditional academia – which frames the West as sole producers of universal knowledge – by integrating subjugated and local epistemologies ...' When, three years ago, the Director of the Pitt-Rivers Museum decided to ask a Maasai shaman to divine which objects from the Maasai collections of the museum had been stolen from their original owners and to repatriate the items that he designated, she was giving practical effect to the idea that modern historical and archaeological methods are no more valid as a route to truth than mystical divination employed in other cultures. If truth is subjective, then every ethnic group may have its own truth, and the whole concept of objective knowledge disappears.

Let me now turn to inherited collective guilt. The argument is that if people once suffered what we now regard as injustice at the hands of our forebears, we owe it to their descendants to make that good. One thing that the study of history teaches us is that injustice as we conceive it has been the lot of much of humanity at most times. Much of the history of the world is a history of the brutal exercise of force: tyrannies, wars, massacres, persecutions. Historically, most people at most times have abhorred democracy, rejected political and religious tolerance, and regarded the very idea of gender or racial equality as ridiculous. What should we do about this now that we think differently?

Logically, perhaps, humanity at large ought to atone for its own past. But at that level of generality the gesture would be largely meaningless. After all, injustice is indiscriminately distributed across the centuries and continents. It would deprive what is really a political programme of its political force. So the call for atonement for heritable guilt is directed against some specific sector of humanity: white people, say, or the British or Oxford University. This is not only irrational. It is also morally repellent. Historically, the idea that particular groups bear an inherited responsibility for some past iniquity has been the basis of ugly prejudices and vicious persecutions.

The desire to visit moral responsibility for the past on some identifiable sector of mankind has generally focused selectively on Britain's involvement with empire and slavery. No one would today defend the worst moments of the British

Empire: the rapacity of the East India Company before its political and military operations were brought under government control at the end of the eighteenth century; the Opium wars; or the Amritsar massacre, and so on. But it is a gross offence against historical honesty to take all the worst features of some historical phenomenon and then serve them up as if they were the whole. The history of the world is the history of empires. From the earliest recorded times, empire and armed migration have been part of the dynamic of human development. Conquest of other peoples has not been a particularly British propensity. It has been an abiding theme of human history everywhere and at all times. The values that we regard as characteristic of Western civilisation were born in the societies of ancient Greece and Rome both of which were founded on slavery and imperial conquest. The bloody conquests of the Arabs in the seventh and eighth centuries gave rise to a remarkable Middle Eastern civilisation, far more impressive than anything to be found in Europe in the same period. The rise of modern Japan as a technical and industrial giant had its origin in the forcible opening up of the 'hermit isle' in the 1850s by the American navy. The European colonial empires between the sixteenth and the twentieth centuries had the same catalytic effect on the world. The British Empire was created and sustained by force or the threat of it, as all empires, indeed all governments, ultimately are. It denied self-determination to its indigenous populations until its final years. Yet it was also a remarkable administrative and cultural phenomenon. Those who governed it were guided by a variety of motives – patriotic, economic, military, geopolitical, evangelical. But at least in the last century and a half of the empire's existence they were also infused with a strong streak of humanitarianism and idealism. The empire suppressed a variety of barbarous practices that it would have been convenient to tolerate, including cannibalism, suttee, human sacrifice and slavery. It brought spectacular economic development, creating global networks of shipping, railways and telegraph, and injecting capital and enterprise into local economies. It brought relative peace, honest administration and the rule of law to much of the world. It built great world cities: Mumbai, Hong Kong, Singapore, Sydney. These things would not have been achieved under the indigenous rulers whom the British displaced. In many former colonies, notably in Africa and the Caribbean, independence from Britain has been followed by chronic political instability, economic mismanagement and relative decline.

Our forebears believed that good government was better than self-government, and that trade and economic development were better than cultural and economic autarky. These are unfashionable views now, but there is nothing inherently disreputable about them. Would sub-Saharan Africa be better off today if Europeans had left its peoples to their own devices? Would modern India be better off if it had not inherited its subcontinental identity and economic infrastructure from Britain? Would the world as a whole be a better place if Europeans had never settled in the Americas or Australia?

Slavery is among the most ancient and persistent institutions of mankind. The Arabs and the indigenous rulers of precolonial Africa were probably the greatest slavers who ever existed. The involvement of the Atlantic nations of Europe is, by comparison, relatively recent. It began with the Portuguese in the fifteenth century and the Spanish in the sixteenth. Britain was the last country to take to slave trading and the first country to reject it. In societies imbued by Christian moral teaching, slavery was only defensible on the footing that black people were not really human. In the late eighteenth and early nineteenth century, the rise of evangelical Christianity in Britain led to a major movement of moral revulsion against that idea. In 1772, the Court of King's Bench declared that the English common law did not recognise property in another human being. The slave trade was criminalised throughout the British Empire in 1807, earlier than any other country except Denmark. Slavery itself was abolished by statute throughout the empire in 1834. For the remainder of the nineteenth century, Britain deployed its considerable diplomatic and naval power in suppressing the practice, initially on the Atlantic coasts of Africa, then in the African interior and the Indian ocean. The polemics surrounding Britain's involvement in the slave trade concentrate on its participation in the seventeenth- and eighteenth-century slave trade while ignoring or belittling its involvement in the suppression of the trade. Yet historically the latter was very much more significant. The seventeenth- and eighteenth-century slave trade was in line with the conventional moral values of the age. But its suppression was revolutionary. It went against the tide of opinion elsewhere in Europe and was against Britain's economic interest. The global consequences were immense. The sheer size and global reach of Britain's colonial empire was the biggest single factor in the suppression of a practice that had existed across the world from time immemorial.

To many people, all this is beside the point. They are not interested in historical accuracy or in applying a sense of proportion to a complex past. Their real concern is with the present, and with those aspects of the past that serve their arguments about the present. He who controls the past, controls the future, Big Brother taught in Orwell's *Nineteen Eighty-Four*. Anger against the past is provoked by a small number of totemic issues, of which race and empire are the most sensitive. These issues are totemic because the position that one takes on them is seen as a symbolic statement of which side one is on in the broader battle to shape the future.

When an issue acquires totemic status, the actual facts disappear from view. The issue becomes a mere occasion for political self-expression. Hence the vandalism of statues and the campaigns to rename streets and buildings. The statue of Edward Colston in Bristol was erected to honour his foundation of schools, hospitals and almshouses in Bristol. Tobias Rustat's monument in Jesus College, Cambridge was put there to mark his generous gifts to his college. All Souls College Library was once named after Christopher Codrington to mark his funding of one of Oxford's great institutions of learning. All three individuals had some involvement in slavery, but none of these memorials and dedications commemorated that aspect of their lives. The objection to them suffers from the same partial vision of the past as the unbalanced historical accounts of Britain's imperial record. Once a person or an institution is touched by slavery or empire, nothing else about them matters, however important or admirable. This marks the extreme point that tendentious selection can reach. David Hume is thought unworthy of commemoration by Edinburgh University because he shared the patronising indifference of his contemporaries to other races. Yet this is a fact about Hume that is of very little importance when measured against his stature as one of the intellectual giants of the eighteenth-century Scottish enlightenment. He was also, as it happens, a prominent critic of British colonial expansion. Winston Churchill has become, in the eyes of a significant minority of the British population, mostly young, a mere symbol of English imperialism and racism. Yet his critics are often astonishingly ignorant of far more significant aspects of his life. His contribution to Britain's survival in the Second World War and the destruction of Nazism are swept aside.

Does this matter? I believe that it does.

The civilisation of mankind since the seventeenth century

has been based on the notion that there is such a thing as objective truth. It may be more or less difficult to identify with confidence but it exists. In history, the difficulty in discovering the truth is due to the uneven survival of sources and to the problems of interpreting those that we have. It is not due to inherited prejudices or ideological tunnel vision. We have traditionally built our intellectual world on the basis that we get closest to the truth by objective study of the available material, by abandoning immovable preconceptions, by logical reasoning, and by willingness to engage with dissenting opinion. These are not just Western constructs. They are universal principles, which are necessary if we are to discuss controversial issues in the same language. There is no alternative route to truth dependent on different racial identities or different hierarchies of power. Yet these basic principles of rational discourse are now under challenge.

The repudiation of Britain's past in the name of a modern political agenda is currently a minority position. That much is clear from opinion surveys. But there is a serious risk that it will become the orthodoxy of the next generation. It is strong in some important groups, notably the young and politically active, and a vocal contingent in the academic world. It is favoured by the widespread ignorance of many people about the past, which exposes them to tendentious manipulation by ideologues. This may not be a passing phase. The habit of reinforcing one's political instincts by adopting whatever facts suit them is too deeply ingrained in human nature. Today, it is intensified by social media, which is a major source of information, especially for the young. But social media is curated by algorithms that amplify views that already exist, suppressing nuance, balance or doubt and giving a misleading impression of a great tide of opinion when the material is often generated by a handful of fanatics.

Those who believe that knowledge and truth are mere

social constructs are almost bound to end up by suppressing competing views. If what we think we know is actually no more than an artificial consensus created by power structures invisibly controlling our schools, universities, publishers and museums, then there is no point in debate. You have to change the power structures, take control of those institutions and create a new consensus. This is what is now happening. It is happening with the enthusiastic support of many of the institutions themselves. They lack the self-confidence to stand up for a rational approach to empirical research and knowledge, which alone justifies their existence. I am not going to suggest that modern academic scholars on the British Empire and slavery are all determinists in the mould of Foucault and Edward Said. However, their treatment of the past often shares the three main vices of postmodernist history: tendentious selection, exaggeration and intolerance of dissent.

In 2017, Oxford University announced its support for the 'Ethics and Empire Project'. Its object was to explore the moral and factual basis of the conventional hostility to empire. It provoked vocal opposition from many academics in the field. On Twitter, calls by a professor in the English Faculty at Cambridge to shut the project down were answered by gross personal abuse. This is the level to which in some quarters academic debate has fallen. Another opponent of the project, a professor of history at King's College London, was quoted in the *Guardian* as saying that 'any attempt to create a balance sheet of the good and evil of empire can't be based on rigorous scholarship'. It is rare to find a serious scholar overtly rejecting the very idea of balance in the assessment of controversial evidence. But it is not as rare as it should be. The fact that his protest was supported by 170 academics in various open letters sends a depressing message about the current state of scholarship on this issue. It also explains why scholars who dissent from the current orthodoxy find it wise to keep quiet about it if they value their careers.

This has an impact well beyond the academic world. Every human society depends for its cohesion on a sense of collective identity. The French historian Ernest Renan, in his famous Sorbonne lecture of 1882 entitled 'What is a Nation?', argued that the solidarities that created a nation were primarily historical. Renan's target was the ethnic nationalism and social theories preached by overt racists such as Johann Herder and Arthur de Gobineau. National identity, Renan declared, did not depend on ethnic or linguistic solidarities, but on a history of collective effort, collective sacrifice and collective devotion. It depended on a consciousness of having done great things together in the past, and wanting to do more of them in future. His definition is pithier in French: 'avoir fait de grandes choses ensemble, vouloir en faire encore'.

This brings one to the great irony of modern debates about the past. Those who claim to be the champions of ethnic minorities are seeking to undermine Britain's past as a source of collective solidarity. They are reverting to morally questionable notions of conflicting ethnic identities that can only fragment our society, obstructing the integration of minorities and undermining any sense of community. The problem is aggravated, in the case of race, by a notion of hereditary moral responsibility, which requires one to recognise an entirely artificial class of modern victims defined by race. The result is a particularly objectionable form of racism that serves to perpetuate grievances on account of past events that have no practical relevance to modern lives.

Democratic institutions only work if people accept the legitimacy of their decisions even where they disagree with them. For that to happen, they have to identify themselves with the wider society to which they belong.

The fragmentation of a society's historic identity can only hinder that process. The problem is aggravated by the intolerant and polemical tone that characterises much of what is written and spoken about Britain's past. The great apostle of Victorian liberalism John Stuart Mill foresaw that the main threat to its survival would come not from the authoritarian state but from the conformity imposed by public opinion. Current campaigns to vilify parts of Britain's history are an attempt to create a new conformity, a situation in which people will not dare to express contrary opinions for fear of provoking outrage and abuse. These are symptoms of the narrowing of our intellectual world. Recently, publication of a book written by the director of the Oxford Ethics and Empire project was indefinitely 'deferred' (in effect rejected) by Bloomsbury, the publisher that had commissioned it, on the grounds that 'public feeling' did not support its publication at the moment. This is the mentality that Mill and other apostles of liberal values dreaded.

We will never understand the past unless we recognise that human beings are light and shade and acknowledge both. Few individuals and no societies have ever been wholly good or wholly bad in any age. This mixture of darkness and light is a critical part of the process by which human societies develop. We can celebrate the achievements of our forebears as well as learning from their mistakes and iniquities. To reject what is wonderful and fascinating about humanity in favour of a monochrome view of the past, dictated by current priorities, is obsessive and fanatical. It is also very bad history. I have entitled this chapter 'The New Roundheads' because the object of these campaigns against historical objectivity is essentially destructive. What their partisans have in common with the original roundheads of seventeenth-century England is a deadly combination of dogmatic intolerance and sanctimonious philistinism. The earlier Roundheads ultimately failed in their attempt to produce a uniform culture in England according to their own narrow vision of virtue. A civilised society should wish the same fate upon their modern successors.

XIII

FREE SPEECH AND ITS ENEMIES*

Article 19 of the United Nations' Universal Declaration of Human Rights requires states to 'guarantee to all people the freedom to seek, receive or impart information or ideas of any kind, either orally, in writing or in print, in the form of art, or through any other media of a person's choice'. Freedom of expression is probably the most widely acknowledged human right in the world after liberty of the person. Most national and international charters of rights contain a provision similar to Article 19 of the Universal Declaration. Lip service is paid to it even in totalitarian states. Freedom of expression is not worth much in Russia or North Korea, but their constitutions guarantee it. Although the law recognises freedom of expression as a supreme cultural value, it is today under greater threat than any other human right. This is happening even, perhaps especially, in liberal democracies such as the United Kingdom and the United States. How are we to explain this paradox?

Part of the problem is that our approach to the whole issue of free speech is still largely moulded by attitudes born in the eighteenth-century Enlightenment when the main enemies of freedom of expression were the state and certain quasi-state institutions such as the established churches.

An edited text of a speech delivered to the Free Speech Union of New Zealand at Christchurch in November 2023.

However, in modern liberal democracies, the real enemy of free speech is not the state. It is the pressure of opinion from our fellow citizens. This is not a new insight but it is a frequently forgotten one. Most of the issues were recognised by the great Victorian apostle of free speech John Stuart Mill, a thinker with a remarkable ability to anticipate the dilemmas of our own age. Mill foresaw that in the democratic age that was dawning in Victorian Britain, a culture of conformity would be a greater threat to freedom of expression than any action of the state. Society, he wrote, is capable of practising 'a social tyranny more formidable than many kinds of political oppression, since, though not usually upheld by such extreme penalties, it leaves fewer means of escape, penetrating much more deeply into the details of life and enslaving the soul itself'.

Tolerance does not come naturally to human beings. For most of human history, what people believed about the natural world, about government and society and about the moral codes of humanity was laid down by authority, usually by people claiming to speak in the name of God. Pluralism and diversity of opinion have only been accepted as desirable for the last two or three centuries. They are essentially the legacy of the scientific revolution of the seventeenth century and the European Enlightenment of the eighteenth. These movements rejected mere authority as a source of truth, in favour of empirical observation, reasoning and rational discourse. But like all cultural phenomena, this is a fragile construct. In recent years, we have reverted to the older, more authoritarian model that prevailed before the seventeenth century, although God no longer has much to do with it.

A large part of the explanation has been the decline of individualism. Mill's outlook on life was profoundly individualist. He once declared that even if all mankind were of one opinion and only one person of the contrary opinion, there could be no justification for silencing him. There have been times when individualism was the dominant theme of public discourse. But today it is widely rejected as a social value. It is regarded as selfish, uncaring and antisocial. This attitude has infected the debate about the limits of freedom, and undermined the case for freedom of expression. It reflects a view of society as a single great organism that must have a single collective belief of what is true and good. This rejection of diversity of opinion opens the door to political action, and to ugly public campaigns that are designed to determine what that single collective belief is to be and to suppress alternatives.

Those who adopt these views sometimes argue that free speech is itself a tool of oppression, which leaves the field open to powerful interests. Few things are more evocative of this outlook than the phrase 'Repressive tolerance', which was the title of a famous essay by the German-American Marxist Herbert Marcuse published in 1965. Of course it is true that in a world of free speech the most powerful voices will be those of people influential enough to have a public platform. This is so even in an age when speech has been democratised by social media. But in a world of free speech what the powerful say will be open to challenge. The alternative to free speech is a world in which public discourse is dominated by a different and more sinister form of power – the power of those with loud enough voices, sharp enough elbows and enough followers to drown out others. That power will not be so readily open to challenge. The idea of a community with a common outlook on the world sounds more inviting than a community divided by ideological or economic conflict. It must be obvious, however, that as long as human beings retain their individuality, their intellectual curiosity and their scepticism, a common outlook cannot be achieved without systematic coercion. What we are witnessing today is a powerful movement to achieve conformity by systematic coercion.

John Stuart Mill anticipated many things, but he did not anticipate the internet. Social media makes a powerful amplifier available to the most intolerant strands of opinion. The algorithms that determine what material is placed under people's noses expose them only to sentiments with which they already agree, thus intensifying their opinions and eliminating not only dissent but even nuance and moderation. They can conjure up instant online lynch mobs. Mill assumed that the pressure to conform would come from self-righteous majorities. But modern modes of communication have undermined that assumption. Social media has conferred immense power on self-righteous minorities, often quite small minorities.

The most remarkable example of these tendencies is the vicious campaign currently being conducted by transgender groups to silence gender-critical opinion. Gender critics believe that while people may adopt the social habits of the opposite sex, sex is itself an immutable biological fact determined at birth. It cannot be altered by medical or surgical intervention let alone by simple choice. This belief is supported by almost all serious scientific evidence and is instinctively accepted by the great majority of the public. Like all orthodoxies, it should be open to challenge. But transgender campaigners do not appeal to any new knowledge, new observations or new insights about sexual identity to support their cause. Their position is not empirical but ideological. Sexual identity must be regarded as optional because they would like it to be so. It is precisely because the case made by transgender activists has no objective empirical basis and little support in the population at large that the campaigners feel obliged to proceed by bullying and violence. Pressure from this noisy minority has created a situation in which the public expression of the prevailing view about sexual identity can lead to dismissal from employment, the cancellation of speaking engagements and publication contracts, blacklisting by ratings agencies, the withdrawal of essential financial facilities such as bank accounts or payment systems, and an avalanche of public shaming and abuse.

John Stuart Mill taught that the only purpose for which power might properly be exercised against individuals against their will was to prevent harm to others. But what we are presently witnessing is a subtle redefinition of the whole concept of harm so as to cover the discomfort caused by having to endure contradiction. The argument is that words wound, especially when they relate to another person's identity or status. Words are therefore viewed as a form of violence comparable to physical assault. On this view of the matter, a university or a workplace where a person is exposed to disagreement with their strongly held opinions must be regarded, in the standard catchphrase, as 'unsafe'. Yet the difference between violence and words is obvious. Violence is coercive. Words, even if offensive, are not coercive except in those cases where they are calculated to provoke violence or to destroy another person's career or livelihood. Yet in North America, Britain and much of the Anglosphere, this notion of harm has captured the universities and the human resources departments of many large employers. They have complaint channels, often anonymous, by which aggrieved students and employees can claim to have been offended. Complaints commonly result in suspension and disciplinary proceedings and may imperil careers. Recent research in the United States suggests that 29 per cent of university professors have been pressured by the university authorities into avoiding controversial subjects; 16 per cent have either been disciplined or threatened with discipline for their words, their teaching or their academic research, while another 7 per cent say that they have been investigated. Those working on any subject involving ethnic or religious sensitivities are particularly vulnerable. More than 80 per cent of students report that they self-censor their work for fear of stepping out of line. In Britain there has been no equivalent survey, but anecdotal evidence suggests that the problem is just as acute. In New Zealand, disciplinary proceedings were initiated by the New Zealand Royal Society against three members who dared to criticise publicly the government's plans to confer on Maori indigenous knowledge a status equivalent to empirical science. The proceedings were dropped after protests by other members of the society. This incident has at least had the advantage of provoking a re-examination of the threats to freedom of expression in New Zealand's universities.

Underlying much of this debate is a fundamental challenge to the objective notion of harm. When interest groups object to someone's opinion, they commonly call for a subjective approach to its impact. Harm is whatever the relevant target group perceives as harm. It depends on their 'lived experience', as the phrase goes. This way of looking at the harm done by free speech is particularly common when the offended group is an ethnic or sexual minority. The desire to accommodate minorities who feel themselves oppressed is understandable. It assists social inclusion. But carried to its logical extreme it gives them a right of veto, an entitlement to silence opinions to which they object. And it *is* being carried to its logical extreme. In many countries, including Britain, hate speech is in some circumstances a criminal offence or an aggravating factor when accompanied by some other criminal conduct. The British police and prosecution authorities have agreed upon a definition of their own devising, according to which a hate crime means any action that is *perceived by the victim or any other person*, to be motivated by hostility or prejudice. In other words, they have adopted a subjective definition dependent on the feelings of the victim rather than an objective assessment of the words used. In New Zealand the same definition has been adopted word for word by the New Zealand police in its policy statement on hate crime. It has no statutory justification in either country.

All of these problems have been intensified by a powerful generational divide. Those who seek to suppress unwelcome views are not all young, but the power behind them is unquestionably the anger of the under-thirties. A mass of anecdotal evidence suggests that venues, publishers, and other media who shun controversial views are often pushed into it by their junior staff. Their concern is not that the product will fail to sell. It is that it may sell too well to people who may be persuaded. This rage of a younger generation against the received opinions and priorities of their own societies has complex causes that would warrant a whole lecture. It is not wholly irrational. The perceived power of vested interests and the inertia of democratic decision-making have combined to persuade many of them that debate is worthless and direct action the only answer. The European and American sense of moral and intellectual superiority provokes attempts by a younger generation to discredit their legacy. Hence the current obsession with the eighteenth-century slave trade, the demands for 'decolonisation' of school and university syllabuses, the attack on statues of past heroes, and the impact of the Black Lives Matter movement even in societies such as Britain where the police do not routinely murder people of colour. The French philosopher Michel Foucault argued that what people regard as objective truth or independent opinion is really no more than the product of entrenched power structures. Debate is pointless in such a world. To get anywhere, you have to break the power structures. Foucault has had little influence in his native France but a great deal in the Anglosphere. I do not imagine that the young enemies of free speech have read Foucault. But many of them act on the same principle. An angry and frustrated generation is unlikely to accept the conventions of rational discourse or the messy compromises of democratic politics as readily as their parents did.

However, the suppression of unwelcome opinion is not just a conceit of the young. During the Covid pandemic, the British government attempted to freeze out opinion critical of lockdowns. The Royal Society, Britain's premier scientific society, called for anti-vaccine sentiments to be suppressed by law. In April 2024, in Brussels, the local mayor ordered the police to close down a conference to be held there by a British political group called National Conservatives and some of their European allies. This was said to be for fear that it would provoke violence, but was, in fact, because the mayor disagreed with the political positions of these groups. The decision was rapidly quashed by the Belgian Conseil d'État, the top administrative court, on the grounds that the conference was entitled to freedom of speech. The correct response to any threat of riots, the Court ruled, was to deploy the police to contain the rioters, not those attending the conference. There was a less fortunate outcome in Berlin in the same month, where a conference on Palestine, due to be attended by a number of prominent critics of Israel, was forcibly broken up by the police, apparently at the insistence of the German government. The events in Gaza after October 2023 provoked venomous confrontations across Europe. In Britain, the police have declined to halt demonstrations in support of the Palestinian cause, but prominent politicians and newspapers have loudly called upon them to do so.

These developments have been a long time in the making and have caught us unawares. They have fundamentally changed the argument about freedom of expression. The

issue now pits different groups of citizens and different generations against each other. The people who scream abuse
at their adversaries from the roadside or from their social
media accounts would claim to be exercising their own rights
of free expression. The impact of their anger is indirect.
They create an oppressive climate in which other people are
silenced and may lose their careers, their livelihoods and their
reputation. The screamers do not themselves bring about
these consequences. They simply influence the mood in a
way that causes other people, generally social or economic
intermediaries such as editors, publishers, universities and
employers, to persecute dissenters. In a world of heightened
intellectual tensions these intermediaries prefer to keep their
heads down. An editor is under no obligation to give space to
people of controversial views. A publisher is under no obligation to publish them. A university or other employer cannot
be made to employ or promote them. They drop controversial positions for a quiet life.

When the freedom of expression of one group is used
to silence others, how is the state to mediate? The law has
generally been on the side of free speech. In the United
Kingdom, the common law has traditionally been concerned with public order and incitement of breach of the
peace. To be criminal, words have to be inflammatory and
intended or known to be likely to stir up violence or hatred
against vulnerable categories of people. Modern statutes
criminalising hate speech have broadly speaking adhered to
that policy. For good measure, the main UK legislation provides a broad exemption for the protection of free speech,
which in principle permits discussion, criticism or expressions of antipathy, dislike, ridicule, insult or abuse. The
British police have proved insensitive to these principles.
They have arrested Christian preachers. They have recorded
as 'hate incidents' gender-critical tweets, tweets critical of

the police, accidental damage done by schoolchildren to a copy of the Koran, even speeches by ministers proposing restrictions on immigration. When these cases have come before the courts, they have usually been thrown out. In one case where the police took action against a gender-critical tweeter, the judge remarked that their conduct offended against a 'cardinal democratic principle'. 'In this country,' he added, 'we have never had a Cheka, a Gestapo or a Stasi. We have never lived in an Orwellian society.' In Britain, there are statutory provisions forbidding discrimination on the basis of ethical, philosophical or political opinion among other things. In a landmark decision of the English Court of Appeal, Maya Forstater was held to have been unlawfully discriminated against after she was fired from her work as a tax consultant because her fellow employees could not tolerate her gender-critical tweets. In the United States, the First Amendment has successfully been deployed against public sector entities such as state universities who sack controversial professors, or public libraries that remove controversial books. The anti-discrimination provisions of the New Zealand Human Rights Act 1993 are among the most broadly framed in the world.

There are, however, limits to what law can achieve. The courts are impotent to protect people against the worst threats to free speech: the howling trollers of the internet, the addictive outrage of the street protesters, or the oppressive self-censorship of publishers, journalists and academics. These things can only be addressed by a profound cultural change that it is beyond the power of law to bring about. Changing this culture depends on you, on me, on every one of us. The only reason that activists try to disrupt and suppress unwelcome opinions is that experience shows that it works. Venues do not book controversial speakers. Publishers do not publish controversial books. Prominent commentators do not step out of line or, if they do, they are bullied into issuing cringing apologies simply to turn the heat off. None of us has to behave like this. J. K. Rowling has taken a prominent position on transgender issues and has refused to back down in spite of attempts to boycott her books and associated films and shows. Because she refused to be intimidated, the campaign of harassment against her has failed and been seen to fail. Rowling is in a strong position because her writings are much loved across the world. Her publishers cannot afford to dump her as they have dumped other writers who broach controversial subjects. Kathleen Stock was hounded out of the University of Sussex, where she was a professor of philosophy, for her gender-critical views. She does not have J. K. Rowling's advantages. But she too has refused to be intimidated, and as a result has become a famous figure. The attempt to silence her has greatly enhanced her profile and increased her influence.

These are prominent figures. But all of us can contribute to the solution in a humbler way by being willing to make it clear where we stand, not just on free speech itself, but on the subjects that have become taboo. I return to the ideas of John Stuart Mill. He recognised that his harm principle was imperfect. What was needed was the courage of individuals to defy the mob. In language that might have been directed at our present problems, he wrote that 'precisely because the tyranny of opinion is such as to make eccentricity a reproach, it is desirable in order to break through that tyranny that people should be eccentric ...' By eccentricity, Mill meant diversity of opinion. 'That so few now dare to be eccentric,' he wrote, ' marks the chief danger of the time.' If, for example, we believe that gender is not an optional status but a biological fact, we can say so instead of being shamed into silence. If we reject concepts dear to particular ethnic or religious groups we should say so and refuse to back down or apologise when they take offence. We have to discuss the unmentionable, challenge the unchallengeable.

The greatest challenge will be self-censorship by venues, publishers, film-makers, broadcasters and the media generally. They do not have to endorse the views of those whose views they publish. But they do have to welcome the diversity of a literary and artistic culture that includes the broadest possible range of opinion on controversial issues. Otherwise their business has no long-term future. The same goes for academic institutions. They are the guardians of free enquiry, and, once it is limited or suppressed, their *raison d'être* is gone. They will say, perhaps only to themselves or in the privacy of their editorial boards or faculty meetings, why should we expose ourselves? Why should we quarrel with our young and idealistic junior staff or students who do not wish to sully their hands with this or that book, film or lecture? Why should we court the unpleasantness involved in speaking up? The answer to that was given by Mill in his inaugural address at the University of St Andrews after he had been elected as its Rector in 1867. 'Let not any one pacify his conscience by the delusion that he can do no harm if he takes no part, and forms no opinion,' he said; 'bad men need nothing more to compass their ends, than that good men should look on and do nothing.'

Free speech is not a luxury. Ever since the seventeenth century, the civilisation of mankind has been based on the notion that truth is independent of human will. It may be only partly knowable, and more or less difficult to identify. But it exists somewhere out there whether we like it or not. We have built our intellectual world on the footing that we get closest to the truth by objective study, logical reasoning and open debate, by what Mill called the 'collision of adverse opinions'. These ideas are not just social constructs. They are universal principles. Historically, they have made possible the phenomenal economic prosperity and intellectual achievement of the last four centuries. The basic principles of rational discourse on which all of this depended are now under challenge. Reason is rejected as arrogant. Feeling and emotion are upheld as suitable substitutes. Freedom is treated as domineering, enlightenment as offensive to the unenlightened. Current campaigns to suppress certain opinions and eliminate debate are an attempt to create a new conformity, a situation in which people will not dare to contradict. These things are symptoms of the closing of the human mind. Something in our civilisation has died.

All statements of fact or opinion are provisional. They reflect the current state of knowledge and experience. But knowledge and experience are not closed or immutable categories. They are inherently liable to change in response to fresh discoveries or insights. Once upon a time, the authorised consensus was that the sun moved round the earth and that blood did not circulate round the body. Once upon a time the religious and social consensus justified the imprisonment of homosexuals, the ostracism of divorced women and the marginalisation of racial minorities. These ideas died out in advanced societies in the face of rational discourse. Today, minorities, racial, religious or sexual, are said to need protection from hurtful words. But historically they have been the main victims of censorship and other forms of intellectual and social intolerance. It is minorities who have been the main beneficiaries of enlightened argument. Knowledge advances by testing conflicting arguments, not by suppressing them. Understanding increases by exposure to uncomfortable truths. This is why no one can be entitled to intellectual safety.

We live in democracies whose entire political order depends on the free exchange of ideas, on an acceptance of diversity of opinion and on a large measure of tolerance of intellectual difference. Our collective life depends on the resolution of issues between citizens by marshalling objectively verifiable facts. It depends on ordered debate about their implications under common rules that exclude coercion and deliberate falsehood. It depends on a culture in which the outcome of our processes of collective decision-making is accepted even by those who disagree with it. That is what is at stake in the current debate about free speech. The alternative is a narrow-minded, intolerant and authoritarian society in which the fear of giving offence or challenging existing shibboleths eliminates the most creative and original products of the human spirit. Ultimately, we have to accept the implications of human creativity. Some of what people say will be wrong. Some of it will be hurtful. Some of it may even be objectively harmful. But there are greater values at stake. We cannot have truth without accommodating error. We cannot live together in society without allowing people to say things that other people regard as foolish, hurtful or untrue. It is the price that we pay for allowing human civilisation to advance and flourish. It is worth fighting for.